HELSINKI

Milla Leskinen
& Jiri Keronen

travel guides

A travel writer with a master's degree in General History, Milla Leskinen has undertaken extensive research in the fields of folkloristics, ethnography, Finnish history and art history. An avid traveller and bibliophile, she enjoys visiting historical sites in Finland and beyond. Her special interests include military history, photography and local flora and fauna. She regularly writes for Retkipaikka.fi, the largest domestic nature and travel media source in Finland, and prepares new travel books about Finnish historical sights.

A freelance writer, journalist and blogger who specialises, among other things, in nature, society and esoteric subjects, Jiri Keronen works by day on cryptocurrency and advertising. His hobbies include reading about a range of arcane topics and composing music. Jiri likes to hike in the wilderness and he is a regular writer for Retkipaikka.fi.

We have taken great pleasure in drawing up *Secret Helsinki* and hope that through its guidance you will, like us, continue to discover unusual, hidden or little-known aspects of the city.

Descriptions of certain places are accompanied by thematic sections highlighting historical details or anecdotes as an aid to understanding the city in all its complexity.

Secret Helsinki also draws attention to the multitude of details found in places that we may pass every day without noticing. These are an invitation to look more closely at the urban landscape and, more generally, a means of seeing our own city with the curiosity and attention that we often display while travelling elsewhere …

Comments on this guidebook and its contents, as well as information on places we may not have mentioned, are more than welcome and will enrich future editions.

Don't hesitate to contact us:
E-mail: info@jonglezpublishing.com
Jonglez Publishing, 25 rue du Maréchal Foch
78000 Versailles, France

LAHTI

Kylmäoja

Harjusuo

Helsinki-Vantaan ✈
Lentoasema

VANTAA

Koivuhaka

Viertola

Kuninkaala

Itä-Hakkila

Puistola

Tapanila

Vaarala

Jakomäki

*Länsi-
Pakila*

Sepänmäki

Kuntola

Maunula

Pihlajamäki

Koskela

Viikki

Vartiokylä

Käpylä

Puotila *Rastila*

Kumpula

Herttoniemi

p. 90

HELSINKI

Kulosaari

Vartiosaari

p. 158

Töölö

Kamppi

p. 38

Laajasalo *Yliskylä*

Jollas

Villinki

p. 12

Hevossalmi

Santahamina

Isosaari

N

p. 204

0   2   4 km

CONTENTS

Southern Helsinki

Central, Katajanokka

Töölö, Kamppi, Lapinlahti

To the West

CONTENTS

To the North-East

To the South-East

Southern Helsinki

THE PEDESTAL OF
ELIAS LÖNNROT'S STATUE

The hidden giant face of Antero Vipunen

Lönnrotinpuistikko
Lönrotinkatu 5–7
Metro: Kamppi or Central Railway Station

Sculpted by Emil Wickström for a design contest held by Suomen Kirjallisuuden Seura (Finnish Literature Society), the statue of Elias Lönnrot, the famous collector of Finnish oral folklore, conceals a secret.

Next to Lönnrot himself are two figures from the epic poems that he wrote: Väinämöinen from *Kalevala* and a mythic maiden from *Kanteletar*. Below Väinämöinen is a stone relief that is hard to make out, but if you look at it upside down you'll notice it forms a gigantic face. This hidden character represents the sorcerer giant Antero Vipunen: as in *Kalevala*, Väinämöinen is emerging from Vipunen's mouth.

In songs 16 to 18 of *Kalevala*, Väinämöinen tried to obtain some magical spells from Antero Vipunen. Buried underground (a symbol of hidden, esoteric powers), the giant swallows Väinämöinen who, after fighting for his escape, is finally regurgitated by the giant (similar to Jonah in the Bible), symbolising his new birth with his newly acquired magical spells.

The pedestal also bears the words from the 17th poem of *Kalevala*, the episode where Vipunen appears: "Sain sanat salasta ilmi" ("Hidden deep for many ages, learned the words of ancient wisdom", translated by John Martin Crawford 1888).

The line has a double meaning, referring to both Väinämöinen obtaining the secret words from Vipunen, and to Lönnrot, who acquired the oral poetry of *Kalevala* during his expansive travels on foot throughout Finland.

During the Russification era (see page 216), celebrating Finnish national heroes was deemed so risky that the monument was unveiled almost in secret, in the middle of the night of 18 October 1902.

Below the head of the gigantic face, a discreet pentagram (five-pointed star) has also been sculpted.
By looking upside down at the giant face, the star lies on the giant's forehead, symbolising his magical power.
See following double page for more information about the pentagram.

The pentagram: a symbol of spiritual initiation and of divine protection

The pentagram is a five-pointed star composed of five straight lines. The *pentagrama* means a word with five letters. In music, it is also the five parallel lines that compose sheet music. Originally, it was the symbol of the Roman goddess Venus and, consequently, was associated with this planet as its orbit, as seen from Earth, apparently draws a five-pointed star every eight years, as illustrated by the astronomer Ptolemy. In nature, the pentagram is the sign of the fifth element, Ether, which occupies the superior branch, while the other four elements (Air, Fire, Water, Earth) occupy the inferior branches. The pentagram (or pentalpha) is also the symbol for Infinity. In the pentagon at the centre of the pentagram, another smaller pentagram can be drawn, and so on. It also possesses a numerical symbolism, always based on the number 5, which represents the marriage between the masculine (3) and the feminine (2), and thus symbolises the union of opposites that is necessary for spiritual realisation. That is why, in the mathematics of the Pythagorean school of thought, the pentagram (the emblem of this Greek institution) is linked to the golden ratio (1.618). Composed of a regular pentagon and five isosceles triangles, the ratio between the side of the triangle and its base (the side of the pentagon) is equal to the golden number.

The Jewish Kabbalah, through its most learned rabbis, considers the pentagram to be the symbol of the will of God and of divine protection. In Christianity, it is the star of Christmas and of Christ's birth, which predicts the Resurrection of both the spirit in the body (birth) and the body in the spirit (resurrection). In Freemasonry, it is the Blazing Star of initiation. Placed in the eastern part of the Lodge, it also symbolises the resurrection, when the follower leaves the profane world to become a new initiate. When the pentagram is shown upsidedown, it generally becomes a symbol of Evil, the opposite of what it symbolises when upright (Good). It means that the Spirit has been plunged into the blindness of Matter and the physical suffering of the human soul.

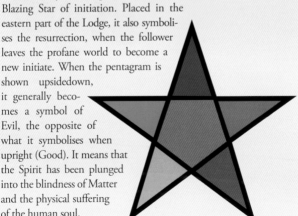

RUTTOPUISTO PARK

A park built on an old graveyard

Ruttopuisto Park Bulevardi

I n the heart of Helsinki, Ruttopuisto Park (The Plague Park) is a pleasant park, popular with picnic-goers despite its gruesome name. What makes this grassy square special is that it used to be a city cemetery; it is still filled with old gravestones.

The ominous-sounding place is officially known as Vanha Kirkkopuisto (Old Church Park). Under the turf lie some 10,000 souls, yet only 48 headstones are still standing. Young people gather around these weathered monuments to socialise, quite oblivious to the fact that they are sitting on centuries-old graves, or indeed that so many past habitants of the city lie buried here.

Victims of the great plague of 1710 were among the first to be buried here, hence the origin of the beautiful park's name. The plague had arrived with refugees of the Great Northern War, in which Russia and Sweden fought for control of the Baltic Sea. A brand new city cemetery was needed when the one around the old Church of Ulrika Eleonora became full.

The headstones offer interesting glimpses into several eras of Finnish history. The tomb of Johan Sederholm (original owner of the oldest stone house in Helsinki) still stands in the northern corner of the park. Designed by the famous architect C.L. Engel, the building used to function as a mortuary.

The last people to be buried here were White soldiers of the Finnish Civil War in 1918 and volunteers of the Estonian War of Independence in 1919; there are monumental stone memorials dedicated to them. The park portal, originally the cemetery gate, is also by Engel, as is the neo-classical Old Church (1826).

Where Lee Harvey Oswald slept on his way to the Soviet Union

The historic Hotel Klaus K in the centre of Helsinki city was designed in 1912 by one of the most important architects of Finnish National Romanticism, Lars Sonck. The actual hotel was opened in the building in 1938 originally under the name of Klaus Kurki. In 1959 the infamous assassin of President John F. Kennedy, Lee Harvey Oswald, stayed in the hotel on his way to defect to the Soviet Union.

During his time serving in the US Marines, Lee Harvey Oswald became interested in the Soviet Union and learned some rudimentary Russian. After leaving the Marines, he went on to travel to the Soviet Union in the hope of becoming a Soviet citizen. Oswald took a ship from New Orleans to Le Havre in France then to the United Kingdom, lying to officials saying he would stay in the UK for a week; he immediately flew to Helsinki. In order to get his visa for the Soviet Union he had to stay a few days in Helsinki.

Oswald first registered at Hotel Torni (room 309), before moving to Hotel Klaus Kurki (room 429), where he stayed until he got his visa and continued to the Soviet Union. He was very vocal about becoming a Soviet citizen; according to the Warren Commission Hearings, he told a tourist guide of his plan to gain citizenship. When Oswald was asked why he wanted the citizenship, he told the officials he was a communist and spoke about the "great Soviet Union".

Oswald's citizenship application was ultimately refused and he had to leave the Soviet Union immediately. According to Oswald's

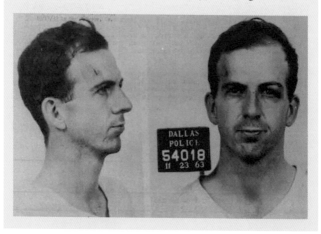

diary, before he was due to be escorted out of the country, Oswald attempted suicide to shock his escort. He was placed under psychiatric observation for a week and his departure from the country was delayed. So he managed to partially get his wish and lived in the Soviet Union (in Minsk, now Belarus), where he married and had a child, until 1962, when he left the country with his family and moved back to the US, disillusioned. The deeds he committed later are well known.

Lee Harvey and Marina Oswald on train leaving Russia.

COMMISSION EXHIBIT No. 2629

CIVIL DEFENCE MUSEUM

A museum in an authentic air-raid shelter

Siltavuorenranta 16 B
Corner of Bulevardi and Fredrikinkatu
09 2782285
museo@hvssy.fi
September—May, Saturday 10am—2pm; other times by request
Free entry

Located in an authentic air-raid shelter with an alarm siren on top (see opposite page), the Civil Defence Museum hosts an exhibition that helps you imagine the bombing of Helsinki during World War II.

The museum includes a War of Continuation-era apartment with shuttered windows and a wartime shelter, complete with an audioscape

of bombs and crumbling buildings. It also boasts information and exhibits about radiation, the protection of civilians, and how much dry foodstuff every home should have in case of an emergency. Among the many curious exhibits are rare World War II gas masks for infants and horses.

Anti-aircraft sirens from the Second World War

The strange structure on top of the air-raid shelter that houses the Civil Defence Museum is an antique siren, one of the few remaining in Helsinki. Two others can still be seen in the city: one is on top of the hydroelectric power plant museum in the Technical Museum complex (Viikintie 1), the other is at the corner of Iso-Roobertinkatu and Yrjönkatu. Near the second one, a plaque (in English) on the wall of Iso-Roobertinkatu 18 tells the tragic story of an air raid in November 1942 that hit a crowd of movie-going youngsters; the explosion killed 51 people and injured 120 others – the highest number of casualties of any single bomb dropped on Helsinki.

Set up on the brink of the Winter War, the 50 or so original sirens could be heard from around half a kilometre away. The system was replaced with a modern one in the 1980s.

NEARBY

Tatar Mosque ④

Fredrikinkatu 33A – 09 643579 – kanslia@tatar.fi

At the corner of Uudenmaankatu and Fredrikinkatu, high up on the side of the building, an Arabic text and the familiar crescent of Islam indicate the presence of the mosque of the Finnish Tatar community, who represent an ethnic Volga Tatar diaspora. The Tatars are fully integrated into society and there are some 900 of them in Finland. The calligraphy under the crescent is a stylised Arabic representation of the first part of the Islamic confession of faith: "There is no other God but Allah and Muhammad is His messenger".

Tatars are a rare historic religious minority in Finland, having first arrived in the 1800s during the Grand Duchy from Russia to trade and serve in the Russian military. Many of them were called to build the Bomarsund Fortress, which still has an Islamic cemetery as a result. The Finnish Tatars founded the original Islamic congregation in Helsinki in 1925, the first to be recognised in a Western European country.

The current mosque dates from 1961 and was commissioned by the Tatars themselves. The building also used to host a Tatar language primary school, which operated between 1948 and 1969, before the Finnish school system reform in the 1970s. Though the Tatar community owns the entire building, they only use the top floors. The other floors are rented out for other purposes.

SCULPTURE OF A FROG

A frog posing as atlas

Agronomitalo
Fabianinkatu 17

In Fabianinkatu 17, the Agronomitalo (Agronomy House) is a beautiful Art Nouveau building built in 1901 by the famous architect trio of Gesellius, Lindgren and Saarinen. The building's corner and sides, high above street level, are decorated with frogs posing as Atlas, the Titan who held Earth upon his shoulders from the ancient Greek myths. Although many see this as mere humorous detail, the symbolism of the frog on this very building may have a deeper meaning: being at the end of the chain of the egg and the tadpole, the frog is a symbol of life, fecundity and creation. Could any animal do a better job of sustaining agronomy (the science of agriculture) than the frog?

The building was originally called "Lääkärientalo" (the "House of Doctors") because several doctors worked there. One of the more famous tenants of the building was surgeon Richard Falt, who operated on the Russian general-governor Nikolai Bobrikov after Bobrikov was shot by the Finnish nationalist Eugen Schaumann.

The firm of Gesellius, Lindgren and Saarinen is best known in Finland for their many famous public and private projects, such as the National Museum of Finland and the Helsinki Railway Station. Eero Saarinen – the son of Eliel Saarinen – is also world-famous for other works, including the Gateway Arch in St. Louis and the TWA Flight Centre at JFK International Airport in New York.

Dotted about the façade lurk more traditional looking gargoyles and winged demons, grinning ominously. The Finnish Art Nouveau style was heavily influenced by National Romanticism and its fascination with medieval architecture.

Poetry on manhole covers

Of all Helsinki's numerous public artworks, the hardest to spot must be the "Epigrammeja Helsingin kaupungin jalankulkijoille" (Epigrams for Helsinki citizens). Most locals have walked all over them hundreds of times without realising it.

Installed in 1999, this unusual work of art consists of eight different cast-iron manhole covers located around the city centre. What makes these covers special from any others are the short epigrammatic poems in Finnish, often humorous and addressed to passers-by. Otherwise they are perfectly normal, working manhole covers.

"Epigrammeja Helsingin kaupungin jalankulkijoille" is a project imagined by the artist Denise Ziegler, who was born in Lucerne, Switzerland in 1965, but has been living in Finland since 1990. Ziegler said she wanted to "reinforce the status of pedestrians as important individual elements of the urban environment." The artwork is part of the collection of the Helsinki Art Museum.

The epigrams and poems relate to the precise location of the manhole cover in question, and also make assumptions about the activities of the pedestrian reader.

Here are the eight manhole covers, with their location and poem (English translations: The City of Helsinki).

TÄMÄ TIE VIE MUISTOMERKKIEN JA RAKENNUSTEN OHI POHJOISEEN.

(*"This road takes you north past monuments and buildings."*)

Mannerheim Square, in front of Kiasma Museum of Contemporary Art.

MINUT SIJOITETTIIN PUISTON LAIDALLE. OHIKULKIJA, KÄVELE KESKELLÄ TIETÄ.

(*"I was placed at the edge of the park. Passer-by, walk in the middle of the road."*)

Pohjoisesplanadi/Kluuvikatu, edge of the park.

OLEN KAUKOLÄMMÖN KANSI, MAANALAISTEN KÄYTÄVIEN VARTIJA.

(*"I am a district heat cover, a guardian of subterranean tunnels."*)

Yliopistokatu, in front of Porthania.

KAUPUNGIN TAKAHUONEESSA NAUTIT NÄKYMÄSTÄ MERELLE.

(*"In the back room of the city you enjoy the view of the sea."*)

Eteläranta, behind the Old Market Hall.

TÄLLÄ PAIKALLA ODOTTI NAINEN JUURI KUN PUNAINEN PAKETTIAUTO AJOI OHI.

(*"On this spot a woman was waiting, just as a red van drove by."*)

Pohjoisesplanadi/Mikonkatu.

PUNAINEN VALOUKKO SEISOO KADUN TOISELLA PUOLELLA, TÄÄLLÄ SEISON MINÄ.

(*"The little red man stands on the other side of the street, I am standing here."*)

Mannerheimintie/Kalevankatu.

TÄMÄ KATU VIE ALASPÄIN RAUTATIEASEMALLE, SINÄ SUUNNISTAT YLÄMÄKEEN.

(*"This street leads down to the railway station, you are heading uphill."*)

Simonkatu, square in between Lasipalatsi and Forum shopping centre.

SEISOT KAMPIN AUKIOLLA, KOLMIOTA YMPÄRÖI HUMINA.

(*"You are standing in a square at Kamppi, a triangle surrounded by the hum of the city."*)

Kamppi, next to the Ernst Billgren's "Meeting Places" points.

"PLANETARY FIELDS" NECKLACE ⑥

Princess Leia's necklace

Museum of Design
Korkeavuorenkatu 23
09 6220540
info@designmuseum.fi
Tuesday 11am–8pm, Wednesday–Sunday 11am–6pm, closed Monday
Metro: University of Helsinki
Tram: 10

Designed by Finnish designer Björn Weckström in 1969, the Planetaari-set laaksot (Planetary fields) necklace is probably one of the most well-known pieces of jewellery in the entire galaxy, or at least in a galaxy far, far away; it is this very necklace that Princess Leia wore during the end scene of the first Star Wars film.

Today, the necklace is in the Designmuseo (Museum of Design).

Weckström was contacted in 1975 by the then not-so-well-known George Lucas. Lucas needed some impressive silver jewellery for an epic space opera he was working on and insisted on getting it designed by

Weckström. The jewellery had to be ready in six weeks, so there wasn't much time. That time was reduced further when Lucas' secretary called and said the jewellery was now needed in a week.

Weckström told the secretary that he couldn't design the piece at such short notice. But the studio was not to be deterred, so they opted to use some existing Weckström jewellery from Lapponia, a recognised brand across Europe.

In 2012 Weckström donated Princess Leia's necklace to Helsinki's Museum of Design.

FREEMASON TEMPLE ⑦

Jean Sibelius, a notable Finnish Freemason

Suomen Suurloosi
Kasarmikatu 16 D
09 6844320
ssl@suurloosi.fi
www.vapaamuurarit.fi
Museum: September–May, Tuesday 1pm–5pm or by request
Tram: 10 – Tarkk'ampujankatu

ounded in 1967, the Freemasonry Museum charts the history of Finnish Freemasonry from its beginnings until the present day, presenting ritualistic robes and gifts from lodges around the world. These include Jean Sibelius' original notes for his ritualistic music for the lodge, and his own membership application from 1922. The wartime president of Finland, Risto Ryti, was also a member and has his own little memorabilia exhibition.

Freemasonry arrived in Finland via Sweden in 1758. But after the Russian annexation, the contacts faded and by 1813, lodge activity had ceased. Czar Alexander I forbade Masonic lodges in 1822, and for a hundred years the Freemasons remained silent.

Finnish Americans brought Freemasonry back to independent Finland in 1922, when Suomi Loosi n°1 (Finland lodge number 1) was founded, with notable members such as the composer Jean Sibelius, who composed the Finnish ritual music Musique Religieuse, Opus 113. Various lodges and organisations have been founded since then, but Masonic presence is very limited in Finland and membership is rarely advertised to outsiders.

MONTHLY GUIDED TOUR OF THE
FIRST OBSERVATORY OF HELSINKI

Visit the tower of the stargazers

Kopernikuksentie 1
02 9412 4244
observatorio@helsinki.fi — www.observatorio.fi
Tuesday—Wednesday and Friday—Sunday 12pm—4pm, Thursday 12pm—8pm
Monthly tour 2pm—3pm (check website for dates)
The tour is in Finnish; private tours available in English by request

On the Tähtitorninmäki (Observatory Hill), Helsinki's first astronomical observatory is not a real secret, but what is less known is that a monthly guided tour grants visitors access to areas that would normally be out of bounds, such as the old observation towers in the attic, where scientists used to spend sleepless nights. The guided tour also offers a stargazing experience of your own in the little planetarium. The knowledgeable guide provides a lot more insight into the former use of the building than a regular visit, which would only allow visitors to see the main observation hall and exhibits.

After the Great Fire of Turku in 1827, Czar Nicholas I decided to move the observatory of the Academy of Turku to the new capital of Finland, along with the rest of the academy. During the years 1834-2009 the building housed the Department of Astronomy. The neoclassical building was designed by C.L. Engel and finished in 1834. Engel wanted the observatory to further beautify the cityscape, and it got a prominent location

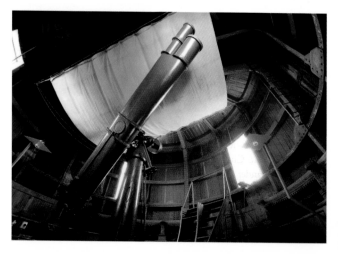

at the south end of the great Unioninkatu axis.

The Helsinki Observatory was among the most modern of its time and served as a model for several European observatories, including the Pulkovo Observatory in St. Petersburg, the principal observatory of the Russian Academy of Sciences. The three rotating towers are especially noteworthy. The middle tower once had a pole that would issue time signals. Five minutes before noon, an oil-canvas bag was hoisted up the pole, before being dropped at exactly midday. As the hill was treeless and bare, the signal could be heard far away, even by ships in the harbour. During the 1870s and 1880s, a cannonball was also fired from Katajanokka to signal midday.

In 1969, during the student radicalism (see page 102), the observatory was occupied and students demanded it be used entirely for study purposes. The university complied, converting the former professor's residence into a library.

When the city of Helsinki grew around it, the observatory became more and more clouded by dust and light pollution. Stargazing became near impossible. It ceased to be in active use in the mid-20th century, and until the 1970s most of the scientific work was concentrated either in the department's Kirkkonummi unit, satellites or in international observatories in the Canary Islands (Spain) and Chile.

The building now hosts a museum and visitor centre, with an exhibition describing astronomical objects, the solar system, and the activities and history of the observatory. The observatory is also the home of URSA, the largest astronomical association of Finland (see page 130).

The observatory forms the end of the Unioninkatu axis, the other end being the Kallio Church near Hakaniemi. Unioninkatu was named by Czar Alexander I in 1819 to commemorate the recent union of Finland and Russia. The adjacent street Liisankatu was named after his wife, Czarina Elizabeth Alexeievna.

STEPPED RAVINE OF KAIVOPUISTO PARK

A quirky and impressive natural formation

Kaivopuisto
The steps start near the children's playground, west from Kaivohuone, in the middle of the cliff with the yellow observatory on top

At an obscure angle in the middle of a foreboding cliff, easy to miss and unknown to many frequent visitors to Kaivopuisto Park (and even to locals) the narrow and impressive gorge is one of the truly weird experiences in Helsinki.

This quirky natural formation was transformed in the early 19th century when German gardener Carl Helm created the steps that still exist today. The steps lead to the yellow observatory of URSA, the oldest astronomical association in Finland.

Kaivopuisto (Brunnsparken) was established in 1834 as a spa resort for wealthy Russian aristocrats. The original spa building was destroyed during the War of Continuation in 1944, but the yellow Kaivohuone restaurant (still standing) also dates from this period (once again by C.L. Engel, 1838). Originally intended for spa visitors to enjoy healthy mineral waters (by chemist Victor Hartwall, whose name still lives on through the Hartwall beverage company), this working nightclub now offers quite different kinds of drinks.

Kaivopuisto is one of the largest and most popular parks in Helsinki. Its cliffs staged a particularly dramatic show in 1855 when the English Navy bombed the Suomenlinna sea fortress during the Anglo-Russian conflict of the Crimean War. City residents, otherwise unaffected by the warfare, came here to witness the bombardment as if it were a fireworks display.

Carpet washing piers around the centre

Washing household carpets with old-fashioned pine-scented soaps (*mäntysuopa*) on a sunny summer's day (usually in like-minded company) is the favourite pastime of many Helsinki residents, who usually use carpet-washing piers (*mattolaituri*), a Finnish institution still prominent on the shores of the city. Most of the piers are managed by regional councils and have tables for scrubbing the carpets, mangles for wringing out excess water, and scaffolds for drying them.

There are over a dozen piers all around the city, mostly located on the beach. They are free to use from May to September. Among the most easily accessible and scenic are the ones in Kaivopuisto, Tervasaari and Katajanokka. There is a handy eponymous Mattolaituri café next to the Kaivopuisto pier.

The piers of Katajanokka and Tervasaari are great for observing the giant ice-breaker ships nearby.

There have been environmental concerns about waste water from the piers affecting the fragile Gulf of Finland, so many of the piers have been moved to dry land.

Here are the remaining ones:
- Taivallahti: Merikannontie 2, at the end of Hesperian puistotie.
- Humallahti: Rajasaarenpengeri, leading to Rajasaari.
- Kaivopuisto: Ehrenströmintie 3, next to the Mattolaituri café.
- Kalasatama: at the end of Verkkokatu, among the construction sites.
- Sörnäisten Rantatie: Sörnäisten Rantatie 19, along the bicycle track.
- Tervasaari: Tervasaarenkannas.
- Katajanokka: at the eastern side of Katajanokka, in Laivastopuisto Park.
- Munkkiniemi: Munkkiniemenranta 2, at the end of Saunalahdentie and next to Torpanranta café.
- Lauttasaari: at the end of Katajaharjuntie, on the right side of Länsiväylä.
- Marjaniemi: at the end of Palopirtintie.
- Herttoniemi: in the manor house park, Linnanrakentajantie.
- Hevossalmi: Vuorilahdentie, on the left side at the end of a small trail.
- Vartiokylä: at the end of Vehkalahdentie, north of Puotila Manor.

THE SPIRE OF MIKAEL AGRICOLA ⑩
CHURCH

A 30-metre-high spire that can be retracted

Tehtaankatu 23 — 09 2340 6123
Daily 10am—4pm
Tram: 3 — Eiran sairaala

Designed by the architect Lars Sonck and built in 1935, the spire of the Mikael Agricola Church has an extraordinary characteristic: since the 97-metre tower could make it easier for enemy aircrafts to orientate themselves, the 30-metre top section was designed to be retracted using an ingenious mechanism. This mechanism has been used twice so far: once during the Winter War and once during the War of Continuation when Russian planes bombed Helsinki. The mechanism still exists but has since been made redundant. It stands as an interesting reminder from the interwar era when the hostile international atmosphere affected even architectural innovation.

Central, Katajanokka

THE STONE IN THE COURTYARD OF THE BURGHER'S HOUSE MUSEUM

A haunted stone that was once used as a chair

Kristianinkatu 12

I f the Ruiskumestarin talo (Burgher's House Museum) is famous to residents and visitors, few take the time to go and check the courtyard of the museum in detail. In one of the corners lies a large square boulder, accompanied by garden chairs.

According to legend, the stone is said to be haunted by the former owner of the house, the eponymous *ruiskumestari* (fire officer) Alexander Wickholm (1823–1896), a notable burgher in town. Wickholm was short, fat and didn't like to sit in ordinary chairs. For that reason he took a liking to a particular square stone he found in his yard, where he often sat and smoked his pipe.

After Wickholm's death, he was buried in Hietaniemi Cemetery. His daughter Augusta moved the stone chair to the graveside for mourning relatives to sit on, but this greatly troubled her father's spirit. The house, without its stone, became haunted; residents heard heavy footsteps stomping around the place, wailing in the attic and doors slamming on their own.

Wickholm's granddaughter Martta understood the cause of all this tumult; she brought the stone chair back from the cemetery to the yard, which pacified the ghost and brought an end to the haunting.

The oldest wooden house in central Helsinki

The building that houses the Burgher's House Museum was built in 1818 and is the oldest wooden house in the downtown area. It is a good example of the wooden cityscape of the early 1800s, with the interior set in a petite bourgeois style from the 1860s.

SHRAPNEL DAMAGE IN PITKÄSILTA BRIDGE

A memory of two wars

Between Siltasaarenkatu, Hakaniemi and Unioninkatu, Kruununhaka

Even though thousands of people cross the Pitkäsilta bridge every day, few are aware of the holes in its structure. Best seen from the northwest side embankment, these scars are from both the Finnish Civil War in 1918 and the Second World War.

During the street battles of the Civil War, a barricade constructed of rowing boats was set up here. German troops bombarded the bridge

from across the strait, causing most damage to the northwestern corner. There was also an incident during negotiations and prisoner exchange on the bridge between the Reds and the Germans, allied with the Whites; a gun was misfired and the resulting bloodbath killed participants from all parties. The Soviet Union bombarded the bridge further in the Winter War and War of Continuation.

Built in 1912 by Runar Eklund, Pitkäsilta (Long bridge) is the fifth bridge at this location since 1651.

Shrapnel is named after British officer Henry Shrapnel (1761–1842), whose experiments culminated in the development of a new type of artillery shell. These anti-personnel shells carried a large number of bullets close to the target then ejected them to strike individually. This method became obsolete for anti-personnel use at the end of World War I when it was superseded by high-explosive shells.

Survivors of the Second World War

During the War of Continuation, the greenhouse glass of the botanical garden of the Helsinki University was smashed in air raids. The giant lilies were the only plants to survive the freezing winter temperatures, and the ones you see today are their descendants.

The nocturnal blooming

Whereas common white (and considerably smaller) water lilies can be seen blooming in most Finnish lakes for a good part of the summer, the nocturnal blooming of the giant water lilies has long been a kind of mystery; an employee of the gardens discovered this by visiting the hall at night, as she lived in the area. The blooming had begun when the plant had around 20 leaves. On the first night the flower was white; on the second it was pink. The beautiful blooms are said to have an aroma similar to strawberries.

A leaf that can bear the weight of an adult

Over 150 cm wide, water lily leaves are amazingly strong: they can bear the weight of an adult person.

THE STEEL RINGS FOR "OLD HOSPITAL" PATIENTS

A harsh memory of the infancy of medicine

University of Helsinki – Unioninkatu 37
Monday–Thursday 7:45am–8pm, Friday 7:45am–6pm; 6 June–26 August,
Monday–Friday 8:45am–4pm; closed 27 June–29 July

Within the University of Helsinki, in seminar hall number two, the so-called Aquarium Auditorium boasts two columns with attached steel rings. They are a stark reminder of the infancy of medicine, when the university was still a hospital. The auditorium was the former operating room, where the steel rings were used to tie up patients during surgeries after they had been sedated with alcohol. General anaesthesia had

not yet emerged and this horribly painful ordeal was the only option doctors had. The hospital was aware of new innovations, however; Törnroth, the professor of surgery, introduced general anaesthesia here in 1846, only a year after it had first been showcased in America.

The building was designed as the country's first educational hospital by C.L. Engel in 1833 and was long referred to as the "Old Clinic". At the time, the study of medicine was still primitive and diseases were believed to be caused by *miasmas*, a particular unhealthy air found on low-lying lands. Therefore, hospitals had to be founded on high and dry spots such as the rocky outcrop here, where the infected air emitted by the patients could be ventilated away.

When Helsinki fell under Russian rule it became one of the major ports of the Imperial Navy. This increase in the traffic of sailors and other people meant that sexually transmitted diseases spread like wildfire. During the 1840s the STD clinic treated more patients than all other hospital departments combined. The clinic for sexually transmitted and skin diseases remained in the building until 1992 when it moved to Meilahti. It has housed the University of Helsinki's Department of Political and Economic Studies since 1994.

Leprosy was particularly common on the coasts of Finland; the first leper hospitals were built here to isolate the incurable. Among them was the infamous hospital of Seili, founded in the Turku archipelago in 1619. Leprosy started to disappear during the modern age and Seili was instead filled with lunatics, orphans and the disabled. The hospital was finally shut down in 1962. The last of the lepers in the Helsinki clinic, two women and two men, lived in the southern wing in the 1960s.

In the inner yard of the University of Helsinki Institute of Social Sciences is an old hospital building, currently used as a clubhouse by the students' association. Though the clubhouse is widely known in student circles, less known is that during the Second World War the hospital was used as a headquarters of Germany's feared Geheime Staatspolizei, the Gestapo. After the war, the building became the ward for sexually transmitted diseases and skin diseases for the University of Helsinki Central Hospital. The ward became a terrifying place where patients were treated with quicksilver and arsenic. The building quickly gained the nickname "Kuppala" ("Syphilis-place" or "Syphilisia"). In 1992 the ward was moved away from the building, and in 1994 Kuppala became the clubhouse for the students' association.

CEILING OF THE NATIONAL THEATRE

When actors represent Greek muses

Läntinen Teatterikuja 1

Painted in 1932, *The Mirror of Thalia* above the main stage of the Finnish National Theatre was the last work by artist Yrjö Ollila before he died of paint-related poisoning that year.

Few people know that of the 30+ people represented on the ceiling, many are in fact the theatre's actors of the time: Elli Tompuri can be seen as Thalia (the Greek Muse of Comedy), holding a mirror and a theatrical mask; Heidi Blåfield, who had recently died tragically young, is the

personification of Destiny, with the thread and spindle; Lilli Tulenheimo is the mourning mother figure, reminiscent of Lemminkäinen's mother from *Kalevala*; and Aarne Ollila is seen as the father carrying a baby. The painting even includes the artist himself as the mason, and his wife Lyyli

as the weaver next to him. Lyyli Ollila was also an artist and actively involved in painting the ceiling. However, the most notable historical person is Ida Ahlberg, represented as Ophelia, dressed in white with her hands held high. Aalberg was among the founders of the theatre and her death in 1915 at the age of just 57 was greatly mourned.

Famed for its architecture, the National Theatre was built in National Romantic style in 1902 by architect Onni Tarjann.

The Mirror of Thalia is not actually a fresco, but painted on canvas. A fresco was considered too slow to produce, keeping the main stage out of use for too long.

The Greek muses number nine in total, and all of them have their own attributes: besides the aforementioned Thalia, Calliope, the Muse of Epic Poetry, is represented by a writing tablet, a stylus or a lyre; Clio, the Muse of History, has scrolls and books, or a cornet; Euterpe represents Music and Elegiac Poetry and carries panpipes; Urania is the protector of Astronomy, with a globe or compass; Erato is the Muse of Lyric Poetry, with a cithara; Melpomene is the Muse of Tragedy, with a tragic mask or a sword; Polyhymnia is the Muse of Hymns, with a veil or grapes; and Terpsichore is the Muse of Dance, with a lyre or plectrum.

A haunted theatre?

Well known for his heroic roles, veteran actor Yrjö Somersalmi (1888-1961) retired from the theatre world in the late 1950s. Apparently he went mad and murdered his actress wife Aili Somersalmi (1891-1961) with an axe given to him by the Actors' Union. He then hanged himself. His ominous spectre has been sighted several times by the staff.

FRESCO OF A FINNISH NATIONAL LANDSCAPE

A beautiful historical fresco in a Burger King

Burger King
Kaivokatu 1
Daily 9am—12am

Understandably, many people who use the Central Railway every day don't venture into the fast food restaurant situated on the right after the entrance. However, they are missing a beautiful fresco that adorns the space above the counters.

Depicting Lake Pielinen in Koli, Karelia, the fresco was painted in 1911 by the Finnish Golden Age artist Eero Järnefelt (1863-1937). Järnefelt, a major player in the Finnish art scene, painted another famous view of Lake Pielinen in 1899: "*Syysmaisema Pielisjärveltä*" ("Autumn landscape from Lake Pielinen") in Atheneum is considered a key painting in the story of Finnish art. He also worked as a portrait painter and immortalised many famous Finns of his era.

Sacred to the Finnish nation, the view from Koli is an official National Landscape, famous since the 19th century, when landscape painters, composers, writers and photographers (such as Järnefelt, Jean Sibelius, Juhani Aho and I.K. Inha) first climbed here and started to shape the image the Finns had of their nation. The development of Koli as a major tourist destination also began at this time.
The three highest hilltops are called *Ukko-Koli*, *Akka-Koli* (the male and female deities in the Finnish pagan pantheon) and *Paha-Koli* (Bad-Koli). The area commanded by the hill was a major stronghold of paganism and witchcraft until the 18th century.

Inside a cave called *Pirunkirkko* (Devil's church) in Koli is a faded poem that Järnefelt wrote there with his wife:
"*Yksi salaisuus, yks henki.*
yks onni kumpaisenki
on kirkko tämä,
sen pyhyyttä muistelemma aina."
Eero ja Fanny 1893

NEARBY
Plaque for Kyösti Kallio ⑥

A plaque on the easternmost wall of the platform area in Central Railway Station commemorates the fourth President of Finland, Kyösti Kallio. Shortly after resigning on 27 November 1940 (for health reasons), he was due to travel by train to his family farm in Nivala; he collapsed and died during the farewell ceremonies at the station. It is said the band was playing the patriotic Finnish march "Porilaisten marssi" ("March of the Pori Regiment").

KALEVALA FRESCOES

Where the originals of the Kalevala frescoes are located

Old Student House — Mannerheimintie 3
09 6128 6450
For tour inquiries contact: kavelykierros-info@helsinki.fi

Although many Helsinki inhabitants have seen pictures of these frescoes representing scenes from *Kalevala*, few people know that they are located on the second floor, in the Music Room of the Old Student House. Outside of guided tours, a polite request to the security guard might get you up the stairs for a look.

Painted by Robert Wilhelm Ekman in 1866, *Väinämöinen playing the kantele* depicts the mythic sage hero of the Finnish epic *Kalevala* playing his mystical kantele, which sounds so beautiful that even mythical beings and primordial gods gather to listen.

Painted by Akseli Gallén-Kallela in 1901, the magnificent *Jugendstil* (*Kullervo rides to war*) fresco depicts the tragic Oidipan hero Kullervo riding to wreak vengeance on his uncle Untamo, followed by a hungry wolf (for Kullervo see page 184).

Kantele

The Finnish national instrument is a plucked stringed instrument also widely known in other Baltic regions. Historically used by the Finnish and Karelian tribes, the kantele traditionally has five to ten strings, though some modern orchestral versions can have as many as forty. In Finnish myths, the kantele is traditionally associated with mystical significance, since it's the instrument of Väinämöinen.

The Finnish national epic *Kalevala* is traditionally sung accompanied by the kantele. The instrument has seen a sort of semi-renaissance in modern Finnish music circles, including heavy metal. World-famous Finnish metal bands such as Amorphis and Ensiferum have used kanteles in their songs, and Finnish luthiers have developed a wide variety of electric models.

The Old Student House

Designed by the architect Axel Hampus Dahlström in 1870 as a ceremonial building for the University of Helsinki student board, the Renaissance Revival-style Old Student House was originally located on the outskirts of the town. Legend has it that this was so partying students would not disturb other residents of the city. The city has long since grown around it and the building is now right in the middle of a commercial centre on the Kolmen sepän aukio (Three Smiths Square). The student board owns the whole commercial block. The façade is decorated with sculptor Walter Runeberg's friese "Kleobis & Biton" and statues by Robert Stigell representing *Kalevala* heroes Ilmarinen and Väinämöinen. The Old Student House was built using funds raised by private citizens, hence the Latin inscription on the façade "Spei suae patria dedit" (The Fatherland donated to its hopefuls). Inside is the legendary Vanhan kuppila café and a ballroom that still hosts many concerts and events. The Old Student House became famous during the globally restless year of 1968, when student radicals invaded it before the student board's planned centenary celebrations, demanding reforms to the university management. It has become a symbol of the generation demanding more democracy.

PENROSE TILING IN KESKUSKATU STREET

Mathematics under your feet

A s you walk down the pedestrianised Keskuskatu Street, you may notice a curious image on the ground; the sun and star-like shapes on this special pavement form a so-called Penrose tiling — a scientifically-generated pattern.

The pavement is composed of two distinctly-shaped tiles: a "kite" and a "dart". Some of these tiles may form a complete sun or a star, but never regularly, as they are randomly created.

What are Penrose tilings?

Penrose tilings are named after mathematician and physicist Sir Roger Penrose (born in 1931), who investigated them in the 1970s. He is also known for popularising the so-called Penrose triangle, an impossible triangular object — in his words, "impossibility in its purest form".

Penrose tiling is a class of non-periodic tilings constructed from just two different tiles following a few simple rules. At first glance they may seem periodic, but by looking more closely, it becomes clear that the patterns occur randomly at larger and larger scales.

Their aesthetic value has long been appreciated. Similarities with some decorative patterns used in the Middle East suggest that a Penrose tiling underlies some examples of medieval Islamic geometric patterns.

Examples include the famous mosaics in Alhambra, Spain, which in turn strongly influenced the Dutch graphic artist M.C. Escher (1898–1972) in his famous mathematically-inspired lithographs. Nowadays, major examples include the Penrose tiling floors of Miami University Bachelor Hall and the Andrew Wiles Building at the University of Oxford.

FOSSILS OF KLUUVI BAY
ARTWORK

The limits of the former coastline

I f you're wondering about the copper lines crossing Aleksanterinkatu, you are not alone. Few local residents know that they are a work of art, marking the site of the former coastline. Designed by the artist Tuula Närhinen, the 8.5-centimetre-wide lines are called "Kluuvinlahden fossiilit" ("Fossils of Kluuvi Bay").

Until the early 1800s, the area used to be a seabed called Kluuvinlahti, adjacent to Töölönlahti Bay. The bay was filled in over several decades to create more building land for the nascent city. Even as late as the floods of the 1860s, mud often hindered the Aleksanterinkatu traffic so much that pedestrians had to switch to Esplanadi to get across.

The bedrock that Finland lies upon was pushed down during the Ice Age by the immense weight of glaciers. When the Ice Age passed and the glacial line receded, the bedrock could decompress. Finland is rising from the sea at rapid speed, gaining more and more landmass as the bedrock returns to its former shape.

The copper line is decorated with the Latin names of different animal and plant species that used to inhabit the long-gone wild shores, with pictures of them on the wellheads.

Some of the names in Latin, with their Finnish and English equivalents:
- *perca fluiviatilis* – "ahven" – European perch
- *bolboschoenus martimus* – "merikaisla" – sea clubrush
- *abramis brama* – "lahna" – common bream
- *stizostedion lucioperca* – "kuha" – zander

POHJOLA BUILDING ⑩

Bears, elves and other animals
of Finnish folklore

Aleksanterinkatu 44
Metro: Rautatientori or Central Railway Station

Known as the "Pohjolan talo" ("Pohjola building") after the insurance company that once occupied it, the castle-like structure at Aleksanterinkatu 44 was built during the years 1899–1901 by the famous architect trio Gesellius, Lindgren and Saarinen. The numerous sculptures on the façade, designed by artist Hilda Flodin, were sculpted out of soapstone from Juva. The bears, grinning heads, devils and other mythical flora and fauna are Art Nouveau (*Jugendstil*) at its best. Some people even consider them scary.

The bear was actually the emblem of the Pohjola insurance company until the 1970s, when it evolved into an abstract logo. Pohjola moved its main office out of the building in 1961.

The façade also displays direct references to *Kalevala* and other Finnish folklore with the name "Kullervo" (another insurance company). Pohjola is a prominent location in *Kalevala*, and "Kullervo" is the name of the national epic's most tragic hero, who dies by his own hand after wreaking vengeance against his treacherous uncle (see page 184). The grinning heads are akin to the Finnish mythic elves *tonttu* or *haltija* that inhabit everything from forests to saunas. They are spiritual beings with a mischievous nature and immense magical powers. The tonttu is a different being to the Tolkien-esque haltija.

The Finnish word haltija could be directly translated as "keeper". Thus a forest elf would be *metsähaltija*, a "keeper of the forest". Elves weren't directly venerated, but the ancient Finns nonetheless gave them respect and offered sacrifices to them, not as an act of worship, but to keep the elves satisfied so they wouldn't meddle in the business of mortals.

Soapstone (*vuolukivi*) is still popular in Finland, particularly in the production of sauna stove accessories.

ANIMAL AND PLANT SIGNS AT STREET CORNERS

A system imported from Stockholm in the 19th century

In the city centre, strange animal signage occasionally appears on street corners: giraffes, unicorns, buffalo, sables, hyenas, pheasants, whales, sharks ...

No, giraffes and unicorns did not roam the city, even in medieval times: these signs are reminders of old city quarters (*Kortteli* in Finnish, *Kvarteret* in Swedish), which were all named after different fauna and flora.

This system originates in 17th century Stockholm, where the owners of corner buildings had to put up signs showing the name of the quarter. When the street names of Helsinki were officially ratified in the early 19th century (due to fire regulations), the man in charge, Johan Albrecht Ehrenström, imported the idea from his former hometown of Stockholm.

The quarters of Helsinki were thus named and numbered using the Stockholm model, and each quarter was symbolised by either an animal or a plant species. This made them easier to remember, especially as much of the population was illiterate. Quarters with major official buildings, such as the Senate Quarter or the Bank of Finland, were not given an animal name.

No new block names were assigned after the 1890s, and the old names were dropped in the early 1910s, leaving only numbers to mark the quarters. The block names continued to be used informally, but eventually fell into disuse. The tradition was eventually revived and new signs were introduced in the 2000s as a memento of the old times.

All the names in one neighbourhood usually follow the same theme: Kruununhaka and Kluuvi have land mammals, Kaartinkaupunki has fishes and other aquatic fauna, Kamppi and Punavuori birds, Ullanlinna fishes, Katajanokka trees and bushes, and Kaivopuisto has flowering plants.

The list includes many exotic animals that don't reside in Finland, such as gazelle, elephant and armadillo; all animal and plant species are real, except the mythical unicorn.

THE COIN OF EINO LEINO'S STATUE

A harmless trick

Pohjoisesplanadi (Esplanadi Park), near Svenska Teatern

In Esplanadi Park (*Pohjoisesplanadi*), next to the "Taru ja totuus" statue (see page 62), stands the mighty figure of a caped man. Eino Leino (1878–1926) is considered one of Finland's national poets and one of its best-loved lyricists. Designed by the sculptor Lauri Leppänen, a personal friend of the late poet, the statue dates from 1953 and hides an intriguing little detail.

Just before Leppänen was casting the bronze, some younger assistants of his (Toivo Jaatinen and Mauno Juvonen) decided to play a trick on him. They pressed a five markka coin into the outstretched palm of the clay model's left hand, as they figured the poet was asking for money (even though Leino was not noted for being greedy). The coin is still in place, even though it's somewhat hard to distinguish in the surrounding bronze.

Realising what had happened only after the statue was completed,

Leppänen considered the prank to be harmless and didn't demand another casting for the statue.

The statue is 4.2-metres-tall and the pedestal includes a line from Leino, part of *The Song of Väinämöinen*: "Yksi on laulu ylitse muiden: ihmisen aattehen hengen ankara laulu" ("One song above all: the mighty song of the spirit of mankind").

Leino was an influential author, journalist and critic whose noteworthy accomplishments include the Finnish translations of classical epics (Homer, Dante), as well as beautiful verses of his own. One of the best-known is his poem *Nocturne*, which is considered the quintessential description of a summer night, beginning with the verses: "Ruislinnun laulu korvissani/tähkäpäiden päällä täysi kuu;/kesä-yön on onni omanani,/kaskisavuun laaksot verhouu" (Translated by Aina Swan Cutler: "I hear the evening cornbird calling/Moonlight floods the fields of tasseled grain/Wood smoke, drifting veils the distant valleys/Summer evening's joy is here for me").
These famous lines are also hidden on the inner cover of a recent issue of the Finnish passport, though they are very hard to spot. Leino's poetry has remained popular throughout the century.

SAGA AND TRUTH STATUE ORIENTATION

A statue that faces the wrong way

Pohjoisesplanadi – Esplanadi Park
Near the Svenska Teatern

In Esplanadi Park, the *Taru ja Totuus* (*Saga and Truth*) statue was created by the Finnish sculptor Gunnar Finne to commemorate Zachris Topelius, a Finnish writer, journalist, historian and rector of the University of Helsinki. Many people don't know it, but the statue is facing the wrong way.

Taru ja Totuus was unveiled in 1932, but when the Second World War broke out and the Soviet Union invaded Finland, the statue was taken away to safety. When the war ended and the statue was restored, it was put back facing the wrong way. Since the statue is old and firmly attached to the ground, changing its direction has been deemed impossible. And Finne himself never complained about the mistake.

The statue depicts two women: one holds the flame of truth in her hands while the other holds a crowned bird, symbolising stories and legends.

The statue was commissioned as an official monument for Topelius by Svenska Litteratursällskapet in Finland, a scientific association focused on Finnish-Swedish literature and culture. When the design of the statue was revealed, it caused quite a stir because of its modern and strange look. An unofficial competing project to publicly commemorate the late author was therefore undertaken by the writer Maila Talvio, who raised funds for a more traditional statue to be revealed before *Taru ja Totuus*. Her undertaking was a success among those with more conservative views of art, and a statue for Topelius, *Topelius ja lapset*, was revealed in Koulupuistikko about six months before *Taru ja Totuus*.

There may be only a few blocks between these two memorials, but their styles are worlds apart.

A time when apothecaries had animal symbols

Eteläesplanadi 2
At the corner of Eteläranta and Eteläesplanadi

Above an apothecary in Eteläesplanadi, a discreet golden statue of a raven surveys the market square below. This figure is a rare artefact from a past when apothecaries were richly-decorated places of prestige.

Literacy was a rare skill in medieval times (and there were no street numbers) so people had to identify the different stores by other means. The solution was to introduce animal symbols as signs for apothecaries, which were also named after the animals. The raven statue is a legacy from these times. When the apothecary was originally established in the 1940s, it was known as *Korppi* (*the Raven*). Other apothecaries included the Swan, the Eagle and the Bear.

In Nordic mythology, the raven is both the harbinger of death and the symbol of wisdom. The apothecary dropped the raven iconography from their name and official advertising in the early 2000s, but the historical statue remains.

This image of apothecaries as prestigious institutions was so important that it was protected by law. According to law, a new apothecarian had to honour the original furniture and decorations. When an apothecarian bought a business, they bought the original decorations and furnishings as well. The law was repealed in the 1980s, freeing apothecaries to choose their own furnishings. Original apothecary furnishings have since become a rarity.

THE FINNISH INSCRIPTION ON THE CZARINA'S STONE

A gesture of good will by the czar to the people of Finland

Market Square
Eteläsatama

On Market Square, the Czarina's Stone (Keisarinnankivi) is a red granite obelisk that was designed by the architect C.L. Engel in 1835 to mark the spot where in 1833 Czarina Alexandra Feodorovna first stepped into the city. The oldest public monument in the city, the

obelisk is a reminder of the Russian era, with the gilded imperial double eagle at the top. On the eagle's chest, however, is the coat-of-arms of Finland, and the stone has inscriptions in Latin (southern side) as well as Finnish (northern side): KEISARINNA ALEXANDRALLE SUOMEN PÄÄKAUPUNGISSA ensikerran käyneelle XXIX. p: Touko- X. p: kesä-kuussa MDCCCXXXIII ("For Czarina Alexandra on her first visit to the capital of Finland 29th May to 10th June 1833").

It is remarkable that Finnish was used; the official languages at the time were Swedish and Russian. Finnish was regarded as a lower dialect that was not to be used in official activities, law or politics. It was only recognised in 1883. After Imperial Russia conquered Finland from Sweden in 1809, Russian rulers wanted to integrate Finland into the Empire as much as possible. The choice to use Finnish instead of Russian or Swedish was a gesture of good will by the czar to the people of Finland. The exclusion of Swedish from the monument is a visible example of how Russia tried to sever the connection between Finland and the Swedish crown. Remaining ties to the old Swedish rulers were deemed dangerous for the internal security of the Russian Empire.

After the February Revolution in 1917, Russian sailors pulled down the eagle and the globe and removed the inscriptions on the obelisk. They were repaired and put back in their place in 1971 (after the Finns consulted the Soviet Union in order not to cause offence).

The origin of the name of the Cholera Basin

The Cholera Basin in front of Market Square gets its name from an incident in the autumn of 1893 during the annual Herring market (Silakkamarkkinat — still a popular event), in which a sailor from Nauvo, Johannes Mickelsson, died of cholera on his ship. Authorities discovered that his faeces had been discarded into the basin, as was customary during an era without on-board toilets. All vessels were removed and guards were posted around the basin for some time.

A cold rock for your sins

Every year at Jaakon päivä (25 July), the members of Suomen Epätieteellinen Seura (The Unscientific Association of Finland) throw cold rocks into the Cholera Pool. This tradition stems from an old myth, according to which the waters became colder because the biblical Jacob threw his sins into the water in the form of a cold rock. Since 1992, as a funny reminder of this myth, Suomen Epätieteellinen Seura throws meteors, rune stones, and all kinds of different artefacts into the Cholera Pool.

PLAQUE FOR EUGEN SCHAUMAN

A memorial plaque for an assassin

Staircase of the Government Palace
Snellmaninkatu 1
02 9516001
info@vnk.fi
Only open on special tours: call or email to book

On a wall on the second floor of the old Government Palace hangs a memorial plaque put in place on the initiative of president P.E. Svinhufvud. The plaque reads: "Eugen Schauman – 19 16/6 04 – Se Pro Patria Dedit" ("Gave his life for his country").

Schauman was a Finnish nationalist who killed the Russian general-governor Nikolai Bobrikov during the times of Russian oppression.

In the late 1800s, the Russian Empire had begun its wave of so-called Russification politics, aimed at politically and culturally transforming the Grand Duchy of Finland. The Finnish press was censored, Russian was made the official language of administration, and the Finnish army was made subject to Russian rule. These years of oppression were personified by the general-governor of Finland, Nikolai Bobrikov.

It was during those years that a young civil servant named Eugen Schauman crafted his plan. Schauman came from a wealthy family and had long been a nationalist. Before the events, Schauman spoke with his closest friend, who was angry about Bobrikov's politics and the lack of rebellious spirit among the Finns: "There's probably no man with the guts to kill Bobrikov", his friend said in frustration. "Some men like that do exist. Just be calm," Schauman answered.

The next morning, 16 April 1904, Schauman knew Bobrikov would

be at the Government Palace. As a civil servant, Schauman had the right to move freely around the building, so at around 11am, as the governor-general arrived, Schauman shot Bobrikov three times: once in the chest, once in the head and once in the stomach. Schauman immediately shot himself twice in the heart and died instantly. Bobrikov took hours to die.

In recent times, the figure of Eugen Schauman has become more controversial, but most Finns still think of Schauman as a kind of hero, and he even ranked 34th in the Great Finns tele-vote in 2004.

THE CLOCKS OF THE GOVERNMENT PALACE

A single mechanism for two different clocks

Senate Square
Snellmaninkatu 1i

Designed and built in 1822 by clocksmith Jaakko Könni from Ilmajoki, a member of the famous clocksmith family (see below), the clock on the Government Palace has a unique feature. Its single mechanism is used for two different clocks: the one on Senate Square and the one facing the courtyard.

Prominent German architect C.L. Engel had requested a clock mechanism from a famed German clocksmith, but had to cancel it because the Senate had already placed a separate order to "some Ostrobothnian peasant," as the angered Engel wrote to his friend.

Yet this Ostrobothnian peasant succeeded and was widely acclaimed for his clock. He was even given recognition by Emperor Nicholai I. The clocksmith family of Könni earned the accolade "Masters of Könni".

The clock faces were recently restored and returned to their original black colour – at one point they had been painted light blue. Restoration work was done by master gilder Raimo Snellman, who used 500 gold leaves. The hands are engraved with the wings of the Russian eagle because of the building's imperial importance in the Russian Grand Duchy of Finland.

The clock has been wound every Wednesday by the clocksmith of local company Widemark since 1920. The first clocksmith of the Könni family was Jaakko Könni (b. 1721), who learned the trade from another smith in Ostrobothnia. After him there were four master clocksmiths in the family. Könni is sometimes called the first "tech village" in Finland, and the seemingly fantastical skills of the Könnis sprouted a number of folk tales, the most famous being *Könnin kuokkamies* (Mattock-man of Könni), a sort of Golem story. Könni built a mechanised robot to dig the soil and work the fields. In some stories, the mattock-man is lost in the river when a servant forgets to turn it at the corner; in more violent tales it kills the Master of Könni himself, who is taking a nap in the field. Grandfather clocks are still called *könninkello* in Finnish.

THE MEDALLION OF THE FORMER ULRIKA ELEONORA CHURCH

The third church to be built in Helsinki

Senate Square

If you stand on the steps of Helsinki Cathedral facing Senate Square, you may notice a square of black tiles on the pavement. Inside the square is a circle made of pyramid-shaped stones. These stones mark the location of the former Ulrika Eleonora Church, named after a Swedish queen. The church is pictured in a stone medallion between the four stone pillars. The medallion features a red granite relief depicting the church. It's separated from the pavement by darker stones and is sited at the approximate location of the church.

A text says "Ulrika Eleonora kirkko / kyrkan. Tällä paikalla oli 1727-1827 Helsingin kolmas kirkko. Här stod den tredje kyrkan i Helsingfors", which tells us in Finnish and Swedish that the third church built in Helsinki stood on this site during those years before being demolished. The church was of cruciform shape with a high bell tower in the middle.

The only Russian czar statue outside Russia

The statue in the middle of Senate Square, by the Finnish sculptor Walter Runeberg, represents Czar Alexander II, who was assassinated in 1881. He is pictured in his officer's uniform during the Diet of Finland 1863, a meeting he called himself. During the Russification era, Finns would put flowers on the pedestal as a silent protest and in remembrance of the "liberator czar". This is the only Russian czar statue outside Russia.

WAR-DAMAGED ARTWORKS AT THE UNIVERSITY OF HELSINKI

A reminder of the great bombing raids of 1944

Fabianinkatu 33
During university semesters, Monday–Friday 7:45am–8pm, Saturday
8:45am–4pm; during summer, Monday–Friday 8:45am–4pm

During the Second World War, Senate Square was heavily bombed by Soviet planes. Some bomb damage is visible on the steps of the Government Palace, but the most interesting signs of destruction lie within the university building.

After being badly hit on 26 February 1944, the main building of the University of Helsinki burst into flames. Among the victims of the fire were the frescoes by artist Albert Edelfelt in the great hall, which depicted the opening in 1640 of the Royal Academy of Turku, the predecessor of the university. The fresco showed the ceremonial procession from the Academy to Turku Cathedral in July 1640. Edelfelt painted it in 1905 after winning the commission in a Finnish Golden Age all-stars competition between himself, Eero Järnefelt and Akseli Gallén-Kallela. The fresco visible today in the great hall is a copy, painted from old photographs by Johannes Gebhard in 1961.

On the fresco appear trumpeters and drummers, with the nobility behind. Next in line are the symbols of the Academy: the keys, the sigil, the sceptres and the annals (*matrikkeli*). The notable figure walking after them is the Count Per Brahe, a major figure in Finnish history. As the Governor-General of Finland (1637–1641 and 1648–1654) he developed the country and founded a number of important cities and institutions, including the Royal Academy of Turku. The Academy was only the third university in the Kingdom of Sweden (the first two being in Uppsala and Tarto). After Per Brahe comes the bishop, followed by the professors, the lord of Turku Castle, priests, schoolmasters and students, all in the correct pecking order. Edelfelt immortalised many of his contemporaries in the fresco, and even portrayed himself in the man on the far right of the central fresco.

Another sad loss was the relief *Vapaudenjumalatar seppelöi nuoruuden* (*The Goddess Libertas crowning Youth*) by sculptor Wäinö Aaltonen, which had only been unveiled in September 1940. As well as being damaged by the fire, artworks were damaged by the water used to extinguish the flames and later by rainwater. The marble relief naturally absorbed it and cracked when it froze in winter. Aaltonen was commissioned to create a replacement relief in 1959, and nowadays both the damaged original and the replacement are on display in the main university building, in a hall and a corridor to the left of the main door.

CLASSICAL STATUE COLLECTION ⑳

For the first art exhibition of Finland in 1845

Art History Department — University of Helsinki
Fabianinkatu 33
Autumn and spring (29 August—5 June), Monday—Friday 7:45am—8pm,
Saturday 8:45am—4pm; summer (6—26 June and 1—28 August), Monday—
Thursday 8:45am—8pm, Friday 8:45am—6pm

In the neoclassical university headquarters, the second floor corridor hosts a statue collection from a bygone era. These statues are unknown to all but a few students and staff of the university. Outside of the Art History Department, most are unaware of their historical significance.

In the 1840s, students of the Imperial Alexander University (the name of the university until Finnish independence) bought the first three statue copies for art history classes: the Laocoön group, the Apollo of Belvedere and the Diana of Versailles. In 1845 the first art exhibition of Finland was held, with these three statues as the main attractions.

Originating from 50-25 BC, the Laocoon group shows the demise of the Trojan priest Laocoon, along with his two sons, after he incurs the wrath of the gods. It was discovered in Rome in 1506 at the vineyard of one Felice de Fredis. The original has lost the later additions at the hands of restorers, but the university copy is intact, making it very interesting.

The last addition was a copy of the elk head of Huittinen in 1912, the only Finnish statue in the collection. This Mesolithic soapstone idol, dating from 6100 BC, was discovered in 1906 in a potato field. The ignorant farmer sold it at a local market for five marks. He later told the archaeologists that there had been similar items before, but they had been lost.

The statues were moved to the main building in 1937 due to a lack of space. It is fortunate they survived the bombing and fire of 1944 during the War of Continuation, which destroyed other original works of art nearby.

When the Laocoön group was discovered, many sections were missing, including Laocoön's right arm. Michelangelo suggested that the missing right arms were bent back over the shoulder, but others believed it was more appropriate to show them extended outwards in a heroic gesture. In 1510 a contest was held among sculptors to create replacements. The winner (in outstretched position) was used in copies but not added to the original group, which remained as it was until 1532, when an even straighter version of Laocoön's outstretched arm was attached. In 1906 an archaeologist discovered a fragment of a marble arm in a builder's yard in Rome, close to where the group was found. Noting a stylistic similarity, he presented it to the Vatican, but it remained in storage until 1957, when the museum decided that this arm (bent, as Michelangelo had suggested) had originally belonged to Laocoön. The arm was restored and the statue group is now one of the star exhibits in the Vatican Museums.

THE SECRETS OF THE NATIONAL LIBRARY HALL

The forgotten symbols of the finest hall in the whole Finland

Fabianinkatu 35
02 9412 3196 – www.kansalliskirjasto.fi
Monday–Friday 9am–8pm, Saturday 9am–4pm
Free entry

Designed by C.L. Engel and finished posthumously in 1844, the grandiose empire hall of the National Library offers many surprises for the attentive observer: there are numerous symbolic statues and paintings around the building, which are mostly ignored by casual users of the library. These figures are a secret sight at its finest – beautiful and intriguing art hidden in plain sight.

The main hall with its wonderful vaults and decorative paintings is sometimes described as the finest hall in all Finland, yet few Finns have seen it. The 26 Corinthian pillars and trompe l'œil frescoes give a fantastic impression of space and depth. The main dome is decorated with four allegorical birds: the owl of Minerva (for wisdom), the rooster (for vigilance), the swan of Apollo (for poetry), and the eagle (for strength and vision). The bird motifs were painted by C.H. Larsson in 1880 during a renovation of the old library.

Four lunettes portray the different fields of science in the main hall: Law (the goddess Justitia with her sword and scales) in the north lunette; Linguistics (classical characters representing Latin and Ancient Greek, a runestone, a Turkish gravestone, a Sphinx, and German, Norse, Chinese and African figures) in the southern lunette; Poetry (the goddess of song with a lyre, elegy with a starry diadem, epic poetry with a sword, fables with a swan, erotic poetry with Cupid, and the masks of Tragedy and Comedy) in the western lunette; and Philosophy (characters of arts and pedagogy) in the eastern lunette.

The exterior of the library has more science-themed figures in the pilaster heads of the façade: Art (symbolised by laurels), Astronomy (with a diadem of sun and stars); History (with parchment and an oil lamp); Natural History (scallops); Law (a Roman headpiece with the word "Lex", a sword and scales); Medicine (the Snake of Asplecius); Philosophy (an Egyptian figure with two torches, a book and a butterfly, the symbol of Psyche, or the soul); and Physics (a triangle and a gearwheel.)

On each side of the main hall, don't miss the two stunning reading rooms as well as the beautiful rotunda and its dome where the books are kept on several floors around the rotunda.

STATUE OF THE WISE MOUSE ㉒

The smallest public statue in Helsinki

Rauhankatu 17
Monday—Tuesday and Thursday—Friday, 9am—4pm: Wednesday 9am—8pm

On the handrail of the main outer staircase of the Finnish National Archives there is a tiny statue. Many visitors will simply pass it by, and for good reason: it is the smallest public statue in Helsinki, depicting a mouse holding a pen. Notice the small ladder the mouse has climbed down.

At the top of the stairs is a second statue depicting the book into which the mouse is scribbling. In the book, one can read a text in Latin, *Verba volant, scripta manent* – a proverb meaning "Spoken words fly

away, written words remain". An appropriate sentence for the entrance to the National Archives.

The *Viisas Hiiri* (*Wise Mouse*) statue was created by sculptor Jyrki Siukonen in 2000. Being fragile, it is sometimes vandalised; if you don't see it during your visit, it's probably being repaired.

NEARBY
Marks of war in Snellmaninaukio

Snellmaninaukio, near Senate Square

The statue of 19th century Finnish statesman J.W. Snellman in front of the Bank of Finland was sculpted in 1923 by the famous artist Emil Wikström. Note the severe damage on the pedestal of the statue caused by Soviet bombing in the Second World War.

Snellman was known as "the father of Finnish markka", the currency in use between 1860 and 2002 before it was replaced by the euro.

MEMORIAL PLAQUE FOR KOMISARIO PALMU

In honour of somebody who never existed

Rauhankatu 17

M ounted on the wall of a large building on Rauhankatu, close to the House of the Estates, is a memorial plaque for the most famous Finnish detective, komisario Palmu.

Commissioner Palmu is a fictional character created by renowned Finnish writer Mika Waltari, who used Rauhankatu 13 as Palmu's home address. According to Waltari's books, Commissioner Palmu is a gruff and grumpy elder officer of Helsinki City's police department who is extremely adept at tricking criminals into revealing themselves. He is only interested in facts, and though he is of advanced age and prone to taking naps, he is extremely capable and able to solve problems beyond other cops in the force.

Though the Palmu novels never gained the same international attention as Waltari's other novels, such as *The Egyptian* or *The Etruscan*, they were extremely popular in Finland; four films were made based on them.

The plaque was installed on 12 May 2005 as part of a friendly celebration attended by several prestigious people, such as actors Pentti Siimes and Matti Ranin, and the director Matti Kassila. Even the Helsinki City's official police choir sang at the event.

NEARBY

A memorial to the trees planted as symbol of ㉕ *Japanese friendship*

Near the Senate Square, along Pohjoisranta, the Memorial Stone for the Friendship of Japan and Finland marks the place where the Japanese Embassy was located during the Second World War. The inscription says: "These trees were planted in the autumn of 1943 by the Imperial Japanese ambassador T. Sakaya as a symbol of the friendship between Japanese and Finnish nations". The maelstrom of war forced Finland in 1944 to cut all ties with Japan for eight years. The stone was "forgotten" and left in a warehouse until it was finally set here again in 1982.

COATS-OF-ARMS OF THE FINNISH NOBILITY

An impressive collection

Ritarihuone
Ritarikatu 1
09 6812050
kanslia@ritarihuone.fi
Guided tours only, bookable in advance, email for details
The library and office are open Monday–Friday 10am–2pm

The Finnish House of Nobility, *Ritarihuone*, was built as the assembly hall for the Estate of Nobility (*aateli* in Finnish, *adel* in Swedish) in the Diet of Finland. It now hosts a library and archives of genealogical information. But above all, it boasts a beautiful and impressive collection of 357 coats-of-arms belonging to Finnish families that were raised to nobility by either the King of Sweden or the czar. Many no longer exist: today, there are 177 noble families, numbering some 6000 people. Nobody has been raised to nobility in over a hundred years, nor shall they be; the last baronial rank was given in 1912.

The Finnish nobility makes up a mere 0.1 per cent of the population, though they have had a disproportionate effect on the politics and

shaping of the country. They numbered just a few thousand, but the nobles held a quarter of the legislative power and most of the important positions, such as civil servants, officers, heads of industry and lords of manors. The majority of them were Swedish speakers.

The Finnish nobles were relatively poor by European standards, especially when compared to countries such as Great Britain. Some of them even worked as farmers. In the 1800s, visiting Baltic German nobles were horrified to witness Finnish nobles dancing with common bourgeoisie in the Kaivohuone restaurant.

The noble estate was never fully abolished in Finland, but the nobility's political privileges have practically disappeared since the reformation of Parliament in 1906. The last taxation privileges were abolished in 1920. Except for the titles themselves, the nobles no longer retain any specific privileges.

The Diet of Finland was the legislative assembly of the Grand Duchy from 1809 to 1906 and consisted of four Estates: Nobility, Clergy, Burghers and Peasants. The outdated Diet of Finland was disassembled in 1906 and replaced with the modern Parliament of Finland. The Diet was reformed from a legislative assembly of four Estates into a unicameral parliament of 200 members. At the same time, universal suffrage was introduced to all men and women above 24 years of age.

THE ISOLATION CELL OF HOTEL KATAJANOKKA

One of the two original cells of the former prison

Merikasarminkatu 1
09 686 450
www.hotelkatajanokka.fi
Tram: 8

Closed in 2002, Katajanokka Prison now hosts a hotel where most of the cells have been transformed into guest rooms. Even if you're not staying at the hotel you can still get a glimpse of how the prison looked — near the downstairs restaurant is a preserved communal cell from a bygone era. This bleak chamber has a rough stone floor and an astonishingly low ceiling, yet as many as 40 prisoners could be held here.

The second preserved cell is a former isolation cell, which still has authentic scribbles written by the prisoners. You can imagine what prison life was like as you close the barred door and take a seat on the cold steel benches. The isolation cell also hosts a small exhibition of old photographs of the prison.

Another reminder of the building's former use is the little-known church, among the oldest in the city. It was built for the spiritual needs of the inmates and can still be visited by asking advance permission from reception. The layout of the chapel was such that male prisoners would sit downstairs, while women sat up in the gallery. Services were mandatory for prisoners during the 1800s and became a handy opportunity for inmates to swap notes. Two guards sat at each corner of the chapel, where you can still see the high green benches where they kept watch over the inmates.

There has been a prison here since the Swedish era (from 1749), and during the Grand Duchy a new regional prison was built on the same site. The older, lighter-coloured part of the complex was built in 1837 and originally had twelve cells, two guard rooms and a church. The red brick extension was modelled in 1888 after the Pennsylvania system, originating from the Eastern State Penitentiary, Philadelphia. This system is familiar from many American movies and has the cells located around the central hall. The hotel rooms in former cells have thick walls; some of them still retain the authentic barred windows near the ceiling. The hotel area is still surrounded by a red brick wall, another reminder of past residents.

Katajanokka Prison worked as a place for pre-trial detention. It hosted such political prisoners as President Risto Ryti, Prime Minister Väinö Tanner and communist politician Hella Wuolijoki. Ryti and Tanner ended up here during the war-responsibility trials of Finland immediately after the Second World War. These trials were demanded by the Soviet Union to hold the Finnish wartime leaders accountable for "definitely influencing Finland in getting into a war with the Soviet Union in 1941 and preventing peace." Unlike other war-responsibility trials of the era, these were not international, but conducted by a special Finnish court. Wuolijoki was imprisoned for high treason during the War of Continuation for helping a Soviet spy.

MEMORIAL FOR MINE CLEARERS

Heroes of the post-war era

Laivastonpuisto Park
Helsingin Katajanokka
Metro: Kaisaniemi
Tram: 8

In Helsingin Katajanokka, on the shores of Laivastonpuisto Park, a strange spiked sphere stands above a stone pedestal. Funded by donations at a cost of around 50,000 euros, this mysterious object is a memorial for mine clearers. The sphere, a naval mine, was erected by the guild of mine clearers who served after the Second World War clearing Finnish seas of Soviet, German and Finnish mines.

After the war, around 60,000 mines were left in the Gulf of Finland. Mine clearing is obviously a dangerous job and 28 people lost their lives in the process, while 35 more were injured. Accidents usually resulted from disarming rare or special kinds of bombs and mines.

Between 1944 and 1948 a total of over 2,000 men and 200 ships were used in the mine clearing process, sweeping the entire coast of Finland from the easternmost parts of the Gulf of Finland to Åland. Single mines have been found in the Gulf of Finland as recently as 2000.

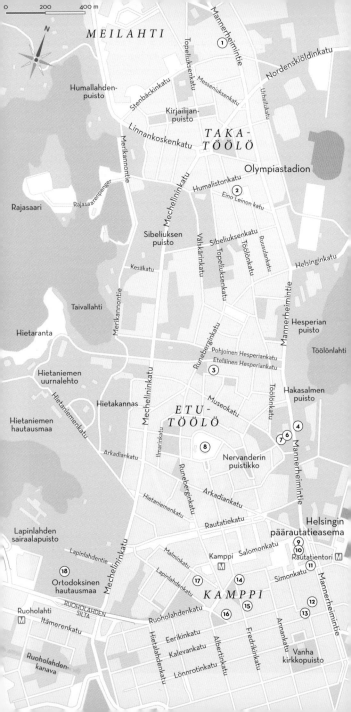

Töölö, Kamppi, Lapinlahti

The city's old customs gates

Mannerheimintie 110
Tram: 4 — Töölön tulli

The non-descript markers that lie on both sides of Mannerheimintie (near the Rock 'n' Roll-themed McDonald's) blend in so well with the environment that many people don't even notice them. They are, however, important features of Helsinki's history: before 1906 they were the western customs gates at the city limits of Helsinki.

The first western customs gates had been established between the 1640s and 1820, at what is now the corner of Eteläesplanadi and Fabianinkatu. Due to the city's expansion, the gates were moved to the western end of Aleksanterinkatu then to Arkadiankatu in the 1830s, before being moved to their present location in 1902.

Their use at their current location was short-lived, as the city limits moved much farther north in the first great expansions of Helsinki in 1906. The location name, Töölön tulli (Töölö customs) and memorial plaques attached to the poles remind us of this past.

The toll used to be five pennies, hence the name of the gate, "Viiden pennin tulli" ("Five pennies customs"). This is also the reason that the neighbouring beer tavern is named Viisi penniä.

Töölön tulli acts as a dividing line in the naming of the streets of Helsinki: south of it, street names generally end with "katu", with very few exceptions, and north of it they end with "tie".

Other old customs gates

Next to Hämeentie Street, near Vallila allotment garden, stands a similar set of stone pillars. These were the customs gates of "Hämeen tulli", in Swedish "Tavast Tull". They were at first located south of the Pitkäsilta bridge and later moved to their present location.

HORSE-DRAWN TRAM

*A horsecar from the early days of Helsinki's tram
system*

Ratikkamuseo
Töölönkatu 51 A
09 3103 6630
kaupunginmuseo@hel.fi
Monday—Sunday 11am—5pm

Located in Taka-Töölö, Ratikkamuseo (or Raitioliikennemuseo) is a museum specialising in the history of Helsinki's tram system. The museum is housed in an old tram hall dating from 1900, designed by Waldemar Aspelin. The building used to have large doors so the trams could pass through the hall, but the building was modified between 1985 and 1992 to serve better as a museum. Today the museum holds many different types of old tram cars, several of which are open to visitors.

An interesting curiosity in the museum is an old horsecar, a horse-drawn tram from the early days of Helsinki's tram system. Most of the horsecars or omnibuses operated in Helsinki from 1890 until the 1900s, but some remained in use until the 1910s. The tram system was controlled by city-owned company Helsingin kaupungin Omnibusosakeyhtiö (Helsinki City Omnibus' Company), the precursor to the current Helsinki City Transport.

Töölö was an important hub for the early tram system. The former hall provided a place to shoe horses, along with other services. The villa district of Ruusula also used to have stables, saddle makers and places to wash the horses.

The Finnish tram system

In the past, Finland used to have trams in cities other than the capital. Today Helsinki remains the only city with a tram system. Helsinki's trams began operating regularly on 21 June 1891. Electric trams began operating in 1900.

The cities of Turku and Viipuri also used to have tram systems. Horse-drawn trams began operating in Turku around the same time as in Helsinki. Turku switched its horsecars to electric trolleys in 1902 and they remained in operation until 1972.

The city of Viipuri never had a horsecar system. Viipuri's tram system was in use from 1912 and remained in use well after Finland lost Viipuri and a large part of Karelia to the Soviet Union. Viipuri's tram system was shut down in 1957 by the Soviets.

THE REITZ ART COLLECTION

An atmospheric little-known museum

Apollonkatu 23 B 64 — 6ᵗʰ floor
09 442501
museo@reitz.fi — www.reitz.fi
Wednesday and Sunday 3pm—5pm; closed in July
Pre-booking recommended — Free entry

The Reitz art collection is a little-known museum that houses the collections of the notable construction magnate Lauri Reitz (1893–1959), who built over twenty block houses, cinemas, cafés and villas in Helsinki between 1927 and 1952.

Reitz was an avid collector of art, rare antiques and weapons; his widow Maria Reitz founded the atmospheric Reitz art collection in 1972 to honour his memory.

The fine and spacious apartment is covered in artworks and antiques on every possible wall and surface. Highlights include the first Bible printed in Finland, the *Se Wsi Testamentti* by Mikael Agricola (from 1548), the first known silver cake server in Finland (from the 1730s), a unique collection of native silverware. Meissen and Sèvres porcelains, ancient clocks, and furniture from several different eras.

One of the most awe-inspiring rooms is the armoury, which boasts antique weapons from the 1500s onwards, including a medieval repeating crossbow — a weapon that could fire eight arrows per minute.

GRAVE OF A GEORGIAN LAPDOG ④

An aristocratic pooch

Tuesday–Sunday 11am–5pm, Thursday 11am–7pm
Free entry

Behind the Helsinki City Museum cafeteria, between the flagpoles on the yard of Finlandia-talo, a little gravestone commemorates Auroras Karamzin's pet dog Camille. The inscription on the stone, in Russian, says: "Shamil, our little dog, Tbilisi 1845, Helsinki 1860". Aurora got her dog when she was visiting her first husband's mines in Georgia: Camille was a little, fluffy terrier type.

Aurora Karamzin: a pioneer in Finnish charities and social work

On the shores of Töölönlahti, a stone's throw from Parliament, the Hakasalmi Villa was built in 1844. It is best known for its long-term resident Aurora Karamzin (1808-1902), born Eva Aurora Charlotta Stjernvall in Ulvila. A pioneer in Finnish charities and social work, Aurora was of noble lineage and a well-known high society belle in the Grand Duchy of Finland. She started in 1835 as a maid of honour in the court in St. Petersburg, assisting the czarina in various tasks. She quit her job in 1836 after marrying rich imperial huntmaster Paul Demidov. They had a son, Paul, in 1839.

Aurora was widowed in 1840 and remarried in 1846 to Colonel Andrei Karamzin. The marriage ended in 1854 when the colonel was killed in the Crimean War. Aurora lived in the villa until her death in 1902. Many places in the Helsinki area are named after her, most notably the Aurora Hospital. Nowadays, the villa houses exhibitions by the Helsinki City Museum.

NEARBY
Grave of a Freemason ⑤

In Kaisaniemi Park, in the northeastern corner of the sports field, next to the botanical garden's fence, is a discreet grave featuring typical Masonic symbols (the square and compass).

A sentence reads: "Lika Godt om verlden vet hvem här vilar alt nog Gud käner hvad han gjort och uslingen välsingar hans mine" ("It is meaningless whether the world knows who lies here. God knows what he has done and the poor bless his memory").

Although nameless, the grave belongs to Major Frederik Granatenhjelm (1708-1784), a member of the esoteric society of the Walhalla Order.

BULLET HOLE ON THE DOOR OF THE NATIONAL MUSEUM

⑥

A battle fought in the heart of Helsinki

National Museum, Mannerheimintie 34
kansallismuseo@kansallismuseo.fi.
Tuesday—Sunday 11am—6pm, closed Monday
Free entry every Friday 4pm—6pm

Up the stairs of the National Museum of Finland, the main entrance door features beautifully carved representations of several traditional Finnish trades. The carving of the blacksmith includes a bizarre detail: a hole in the head of the craftsman. The hole is in fact the result of a bullet fired during the Finnish Civil War by the Reds from the old Russian barracks (Turun kasarmi) located on the site that now houses Lasipalatsi. If you look at the other side of the door, you will notice that the bullet went through the door ...

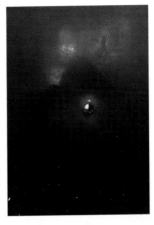

The area had been used for military training even back in the Swedish era, which is how it acquired its name, Kamppi (Campementsplats). These barracks, which saw heavy fighting, eventually burned down; the ruins were demolished after the war.

The only remaining building is the barracks' yellow economic building, which now houses restaurants and pubs. It served as the city's bus terminal between 1935 and 2005.

NEARBY

A rare underground cemetery　　⑦

In the basement of the museum are a group of reddish human skulls, originating from the so-called sacrificial spring of Levänluhta in Isokyrö, Ostrobothnia. Folk tales recount that human skulls and bones were harvested there for centuries. The mystical atmosphere was further enhanced by the gruesome blood-red ferrous water (containing iron). The skulls from the museum, some of the 98 found in total, still bear much of this colouring. For a long time the skulls were thought to have been from ancient victims of violence, drowned in a swamp like many famous "bog bodies" in Germanic and Celtic lands. More sound guesses linked them to a relatively modern massacre, the burial place of 16th-century Cudgel War (Nuijasota) victims. Recently, historians have come to believe that Levänluhta was actually an underwater cemetery, and a completely unique one: the site was originally a small lake used as a burial place between the fourth and eighth centuries. Underwater burial is extremely rare, almost unheard of in the Old World, and similar methods have been used by only a few ancient Native Americans in the Everglades, Florida.

THE "BIAFRA" GRAFFITI OF TEMPPELIAUKIO CHURCH

Radical graffiti from the 1960s

Lutherinkatu 3
09 2340 6320 — toolo.srk@evl.fi
Daily 10am–5pm, entrance to the cellar by request

If requested in advance, a kind custodian will escort you to the dusty cellar of the Temppeliaukio Church (The Church in the Rock), where you can see that this magnificent temple did not always have a peaceful existence. Painted on the bedrock wall, graffiti spelling out the word "Biafra" acts as a reminder of the difficult early days of the church.

Called an "anti-Devil defence bunker" or a "rock mosque" by the Fin-nish media, Temppeliaukio Church was criticised from the start for its high cost. In July of 1968 a group of university students from the Students' Christian Association attacked the construction yard, defacing its foundations with eleven pieces of graffiti that spelled "Biafra"; they wanted to highlight the hypocrisy between the contemporary Biafran famine crisis and the building of yet another expensive church. This graffiti was one of the first modern examples in Finland and the first to gain wide media attention.

Though Temppeliaukio Church was built in 1969, its history stretches back to before Finnish independence; a site for the church was planned as early as 1906, and in 1932 a competition was held to come up with a design. The results didn't satisfy officials of the Lutheran church and they tried to hold a second competition. The Winter War put an end to their plans, but a third competition was finally held in 1961, won by architects Timo and Tuomo Suomalainen.

The Temppeliaukio Church is a unique and spectacular piece of architecture; it resembles a large dome mined inside a magnificent cave. A crack in the rock from the last great ice age serves as the altar relief. The altar itself is made of smooth granite. The church has no bells; instead, an electric audio system plays a unique piece of bell music composed by professor Taneli Kuusisto.

Biafra is an oil-rich Christian region of Nigeria, situated in the south-east of the country. It became famous between 1967 and 1970 when, following an ethnic civil war, it announced secession from Nigeria. Two million Biafrans died of starvation as a result of that war.

THE WILLOW OF LASIPALATSI

The giant's offspring

Salomonkatu
Next to the Bio Rex cinema in Lasipalatsi

The willow of Lasipalatsi (Lasipalatsin salava) was a famous old tree (isoriippasalava species — Salix x rubens) that was growing just outside the Lasipalatsi building. It was originally part of a tree alley planted in the 1830s by Russians on the future Salomonkatu Street to frame a Turku barracks.

Most of the trees in the alley fell down during a violent storm in August 1890, but this one survived and was protected as a natural monument in 1924. At that time it was already the most famous tree in Helsinki.

After the Lasipalatsi building was built in the 1930s, people began calling the tree "the willow of Lasipalatsi". But when the long-distance bus station in the former barracks grew busier in the 1980s, many drivers considered the tree an obstacle and demands were made for it to be cut down.

In December 2003 the tree fell in another heavy storm. The willow was deeply mourned by Helsinkians of all ages. But fortunately, the tree had many shoots, and in 2011 one of them was planted on the same site. Not yet as massive as its predecessor, it is easy to miss.

The young willow is now protected by a sturdy metal grille that bears a plaque detailing its history.

The stump of the old willow has been transferred to the man-made fell in Vuosaari (see page 202) as a strange relic for pilgrimage in this far-off location.

BIO REX PROJECTION BOOTH STAIRS

Memento from the era of nitrate films

Mannerheimintie 22–24
www.korjaamokino.fi

Many passers-by have wondered about the purpose of a strange staircase on the inner courtyard wall of Lasipalatsi. These seemingly pointless stairs appear in the middle of the wall and connect two mysterious doors.

The staircase dates from 1936 and belongs to the adjacent Bio Rex movie theatre complex. During the era of highly flammable nitrate films, the stairs provided the only safe option of isolating the dangerous and potentially auto-igniting film reels from the rest of the theatre.

A tragic chapter in Finnish movie-going history occured at the Imatra movie theatre in Tampere on 23 October 1927. During a screening of *Wages of Virtue* (1924), ten nitrate film reels self-ignited in the projection booth, starting a catastrophic fire that killed 21 people and injured 27 others. After the tragedy, regulations concerning fire safety in movie theatres were tightened; the projection booth now had to be both isolated from the rest of the theatre and have its own emergency exit. This led to the design of the external staircase of the Bio Rex.

Bio Rex (under the name Korjaamo Kino) still shows rare and independent films during weekends. Though films are now digital, the external stairs are still the only way up to the projector room and the current operators have to use them, rain or shine.

Lasipalatsi is one of the most notable functionalist buildings in the city. It replaced the Turku barracks, which were destroyed in a fire in the Civil War. Built in 1936, Lasipalatsi was designed by three young architects, Viljo Revell, Heimo Riihimäki and Niilo Kokko. At the time of the opening, Bio Rex was among the biggest of its kind in Finland, and many premieres of notable Finnish classics were shown here. Lasipalatsi was originally meant to be temporary, but plans to tear it down were postponed for decades. The building fell into disrepair but was eventually saved, renovated and protected as a masterpiece of Finnish functionalism.

ANIMAL TRACKS HIDDEN ON THE PAVEMENT

An artwork that symbolises our close connection to nature

Between Lasipalatsi and Forum shopping centre, at the crossroads of Simonkatu and Mannerheimintie

Just outside the Forum shopping centre on Simonkatu there is a busy corner where people rush between Kamppi and the railway station. You can easily miss the intriguing work of art right under your feet, but take a look down and you'll see 20 bronze tiles spread around the area among the regular paving blocks. Dating from 2000, these tiles are actually a sculpture called *Hiljaisuuden jalanjäljet* (*Footprints of Silence*) by Andy Best and Merja Puustinen.

The tiles are decorated with impressions of footprints from various

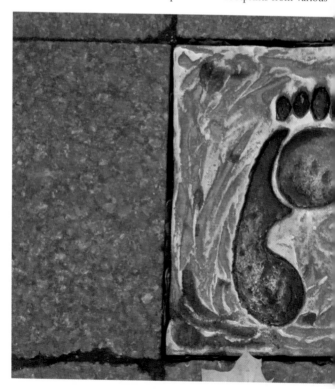

animals that once walked here, when Helsinki was just a woodland. The tiles also include the names of the species: wolverine, red squirrel, otter, pine marten, wolf, beaver, elk, bear, various species of deer, red fox, wild boar, least weasel, European mink, lynx, badger, capercaillie, grouse and crane. Some of these species are already extinct or endangered in Finland; a few still roam inside the city limits.

The artist couple who produced this vivid memento of disappearing wildlife got the footprints from animals living in Ranua and Ähtäri Zoos, which concentrate on native Finnish species. The artwork symbolises the close connection to nature and reminds us that the time when we lived in the wilderness is not far behind.

A practical joke by the students of the Helsinki University of Technology (now Aalto University, see page 147) is now permanently included in the artwork. It shows the footprint of a wild *teekkari* (student of technology), which apparently once roamed the ancient forests here. The "scientific" explanation text says: "Teekkari / Teknolog / Ubi bene ibi polytechnic".

YRJÖNKATU NATURIST SWIMMING HALL

The oldest swimming pool in the country, open for naturists

Yrjönkatu 21 B — 00120 Helsinki
09 310 8740
www.hel.fi/www/helsinki/fi/kulttuuri-ja-vapaaaika/liikunta/sisaliikuntapaikat/
uimahallit/yrjonkadun-uimahalli

Built in 1928, the Yrjönkatu swimming hall is the oldest pool in the country. Inspired by Stockholm's Centralbadet, its interior is a good example of then popular classicism.

Swimwear has always been optional at the hall and this tradition prevails today, hence this is a popular place for nudists. Swimwear has actually only been permitted at all since 2001: before that, this was strictly a naturist place.

Men and women swim on different days: Mondays, Wednesdays and Fridays are reserved solely for women, while Tuesdays, Thursdays and Saturdays are for men. The staff on any day can be of either gender.

One of the specialities of the Yrjönkatu swimming hall is its exclusive and unique mead. You can also reserve a VIP ticket to get to the upper floor, where you can take a nap in one of the private rooms.

Despite its history and beauty, Yrjönkadun uimahalli is a regular city-administrated swimming hall, which keeps the prices low compared to actual spas.

The swimming hall was designed by the architect Väinö Vähäkallio, whose name rings a sinister bell in the minds of many older Finns: in 1928 Vähäkallio bought Kytäjä Manor in nearby Hyvinkää, which is said to be cursed. The manor's recent history includes numerous suicides, deadly diseases and accidental deaths by gunfire. The most famous dark deed is the 1972 murder of three teenage boys camping in the grounds. The lord of the manor, Kai Kustaa Vähäkallio (the architect's grandson), committed suicide after serving his sentence for the crime. At the time of research, the historic mansion has fallen into disrepair and is set to be pulled down for rebuilding.

THE ZEPPELIN MAST OF SOKOS HOTEL TORNI

The Graf Zeppelin never made it to Hotelli Torni

Yrjönkatu 26

Hotelli Torni (The Tower Hotel) is a skyscraper hotel that opened in 1931. Standing at 69.5 metres, Torni was the tallest building in the country until 1976, when the oil company Neste completed its new headquarters in Espoo.

The bar at the top of the hotel has an impressive panoramic view of the city and a very interesting feature: a mast on its roof that was original-ly built for docking the German Graf Zeppelin airship. Hotel guests travel-ling on the airship would pop down to the bar through a special hatch. Despite this intriguing design, the Graf Zeppelin never made it to Ho-telli Torni, but the hatch to the roof remains intact.

A history of Soviet occupation

Hotelli Torni became an important place of political intrigue in the first year that it was built. In 1932 the Mäntsälä rebellion occurred when a radical anti-communist group called Lapuan liike attempted a coup against the Finnish government. The liberal right-wing party Edistyspuolue created its own forces to support the government and oppose the radical movement. These forces, known by the name of Isänmaan ja Lain Puolesta (For the Fatherland and the law), were co-ordinated from Hotelli Torni's room 310 by Major Into Auer. Af-ter the failed coup, Lapuan liike was disbanded by the government. The hotel was again at the centre of political events when the Winter War between Finland and the Soviet Union broke out in 1939. It became the hub for international media as its guests included journa-lists from around the world. Their reports told the world the David and Goliath story of a small nation fighting against the invasion of the far greater Soviet Union.

During the War of Continuation the hotel became the headquarters of the Wehrmacht, which continued to operate from there until the last days of the conflict in 1944. After the war the victorious Allies established the Control Commission, led by the Soviet Union, and chose Hotelli Torni as its operating HQ. From there Soviet officials and spies could exert tight control over Finnish politics. The Control Commission operated in Hotelli Torni until 1947.

In 1959 the future assassin of President John F. Kennedy, Lee Har-vey Oswald, stayed in the hotel on his way to defect to the Soviet Union. See page 18 for more information on Lee Harvey Oswald in Helsinki.

THE MYSTERY OF THE TRANSFORMERS LOGOS

Alien symbols on the tram tracks of Helsinki

Various tram tracks in Helsinki

I f you look carefully at the tram tracks at the corner of Urho Kekkosen katu and Fredrikinkatu, you'll see an engraving that looks like the logo of the Transformers toy brand that became popular in the 1980s, and even more popular when director Michael Bay released his movies based on the toys. The films are about two robotic alien races, the good Autobots and the evil Decepticons, who fight for dominance of the universe – Helsinki has the symbols of both races.

Nobody knows for sure when the engraving first appeared, but there are claims and photos dating back to at least 2008. Other theories suggest that the logo was etched in 2010 when major maintenance work was done on the tram intersection.

According to Helsinki City Transport rail unit director Pekka Sirviö, the logos were either etched secretly at Helsinki City Transport's own repair shop or they were already there when the rails arrived in Finland. As it would be too expensive to replace the rails, the symbols will probably remain for some time ...

Other Transformers symbols in Helsinki

A Decepticon symbol is at an intersection grid on a tram rail at the crossing of Frederikinkatu and Urho Kekkosen katu in Kamppi district. Beside the logo is etched the year 2011 — the year the tracks were renovated, but also the year the movie *Transformers: Dark of the Moon* was released.

Another Autobot symbol is engraved on a tram rail in Kluuvi district at the intersection of Aleksanterinkatu and Mikonkatu.

LUTHERAN CHURCH

15

A church turned nightclub, turned church again

Fredrikinkatu 42
09 251390
Mass on Sunday 4pm–5:30pm

Close to Kamppi, the Lutheran Church was built in 1894. Since then, it has served as almost everything possible: a café, a wrestling arena, a heavy metal nightclub and, yes, a church.

The original chapel (built in 1878 and designed by Theodor Höijer) stood close to where the Lutheran church now stands. When its attendance grew, the Lutheran church was built. Designed by Karl August Wrede in a traditional Gothic style, the chapel has been expanded several times ever since.

Though the original chapel has disappeared, the Lutheran church remains, despite enduring some rough times. After suffering heavy bomb damage during the Winter War, the church was restored, but attendance dwindled as other new churches were built. In 1986 a group of teens tried to squat in the all-but-deserted church to protest against the poor housing situation in Helsinki. Later, the church came under the protection of law due to its historical value.

In 1989 the church was sold to financial company Sampo and construction company Polaris. The first restaurant, Cafe Barock, was established in the old church in 1990. Since then it has seen many different restaurants, nightclubs and events. There has been a hip-hop club, a nightclub that held pro wrestling events, and a heavy metal bar inspired by Dante's inferno.

In 2014 the church was restored. The design is "modern meets Gothic". Unlike most Lutheran churches, the altar doesn't have the traditional altar rail; instead, a text is engraved on the floor: "Jeesuksen Kristuksen ruumis, teidän puolestanne annettu ja vuodatettu" ("The blood of Jesus Christ, bled for you and given for you").

16

STATUE OF ARVO "ARSKA" PARKKILA

A statue for a homeless alcoholic

Lapinlahden puistikko

In a small triangular park of Lapinlahden puistikko stands a statue of a rugged man reaching out with an open hand. This statue by Oskar Milans, named *A Man Rises from Ashcan*, depicts Arvo "Arska" Parkkila, a homeless alcoholic and hobo who dedicated his life to helping others sharing his fate. After sobering up, Parkkila gave vagrants, drifters and drunks food, shelter and work.

Parkkila knew nothing of his biological family except that his father was a drunk. When Parkkila was four he was taken in by a family with strict Christian values and discipline. He was forced to be a model child — even playing was prohibited.

After leaving his childhood home, Parkkila took his first sips. Even though alcohol was outlawed by prohibition, it was easy to obtain. Parkkila soon began regular drinking. Arska worked at several different jobs and even married. The marriage bore Arska a son, whom he met decades later in the 1970s.

In the Winter War, Arska served as a corporal and leader of a horse squad under the command of General Erik Heinrichs. Arska survived the first war without serious harm, but suffered a leg injury in the battles of the War of Continuation and suffered shell shock in the bombings. He returned from the war a man broken in both flesh and spirit.

Soon after the war he lost his home and wife and sank deeper into the caress of booze. He lived a vagabond life, drifting aimlessly from place to place, sleeping in old bomb shelters and in the crypts of Agricola church. He drank alcohol substitutes — colognes and cleaning fluid — and took several kinds of pills. His friends knew him as a sort of father figure for the hobo community, someone who organised things and made sure that everyone got their liquids.

In the Christmas of 1959 Parkkila had a revelation described as almost religious by his comrades. Though his nerves had been severely damaged, he threw away his crutches and swore "Arska, never again!" Since that day he never took another drink in his life.

Arska became a helper of alcoholics and the homeless. With his second wife Olga he rented a coal cellar to serve as a shelter. They helped 50 to 100 people daily, which was a lot, since in those days Helsinki had about 600 homeless. A few years later Arska was also influential in setting up the "Lepakkoluola" ("Bat Cave") shelter for the homeless.

PRIVATE VISIT TO THE HELSINKI SYNAGOGUE

A great way to better understand Jewish traditions

Malminkatu 26 – Kamppi
09 5860310
srk@jchelsinki.fi
30-minute guided tour Monday–Thursday 10am and 2pm in Finnish, with Swedish, English and Hebrew available on demand (ID required)

The Helsinki Synagogue in Kamppi is one of the only two Jewish synagogues in Finland. Though many are familiar with the distinctive dome of this 1906 building, few ever venture inside. However, it is possible to book a tour of the building with a highly knowledgeable representative of the local Jewish community. This is a great way to better understand Jewish traditions, specifically the Jews in Finland.

Highlights of the tour include the opening of the sanctum sanctorum, the Torah Ark, which is decorated with wooden lions dating from 17th century Poland. The Ark itself is a donation from New York.

Most of the scrolls are robed in fine fabric mantels, called the "Mantle of Law". But perhaps the most moving is the worn mantel of the Torah scroll, which accompanied Finnish Jewish soldiers to the front in the Winter War.

Fallen Finnish Jewish soldiers have a memorial plaque listing their names in the downstairs corridor of the synagogue.

Helsinki also boasts a group of *Stolpersteins* (stumbling stones), commemorating an extradited Jewish family. The brass plates are located in Munkkiniemen Puistotie, where the refugee family (Georg, Janka and Franz Olof Kollman) lived before being handed to the Nazis in 1942. Georg, the father, survived, but his wife and son died in Auschwitz. The Stolpersteins were cast by German artist Gunter Demning, whose project now covers over 67,000 plates in 22 countries.

OLD JEWISH CEMETERY

A forgotten Jewish graveyard

Lapinlahdenpolku 6
Daily 7am—10pm
Metro: Ruoholahti

In a leafy part of Lapinlahti, near an equally interesting Tatar Muslim graveyard, the Old Jewish Cemetery is an atmospheric forgotten graveyard containing about 80 tombs. Volunteers or staff of the Jewish Congregation of Helsinki occasionally cut the grass or rake the leaves, but it's more likely you'll have the whole place to yourself, which only adds to the charm of the visit.

With its last burial in the early 1910s, the cemetery is often covered by moss, and few of the graves have the customary small pebbles placed on

them: the people buried here are now mostly as forgotten as the place itself. Dating back to at least 1830-1840, the cemetery was slowly replaced by the new Jewish cemetery in Hietaniemi, built in 1895.

Jews buried here are most likely of Russian heritage, those who had migrated to Finland while being conscripted to the Imperial Russian Army. Some of them served in Finland and settled down permanently. Many of the current Finnish Jews are descendants of these Imperial soldiers.

The forgotten origin of the word "narinkka"

The main pedestrian plaza in nearby Kamppi was the site of a market run by Jewish merchants from the late 19th century until 1929. It has now been officially named Narinkka Square (Finnish: *Narinkkatori*, Swedish: *Narinken*). The name of the Jewish market has its origins in Russian, as many of the Jews originated from Russia: "на рынке" (na rinke), which means "on the market". The Finnish habitants began to call the place "narinkka" and the name stuck. Today very few people know the original meaning of the word.

"We do not have a Jewish Question"

The first Jews settled in Finland early in the 1800s, most of them after being posted there while serving in the Russian Imperial Army. The first synagogue was established in Suomenlinna in 1830 for these Jewish soldiers, originally in an old stable. The current brethren of the Helsinki Synagogue are mostly descendants of these Imperial soldiers. Finland was allied with Nazi Germany but the Jewish population of Finland did not suffer heavy persecution as in other European countries. When Heinrich Himmler, the architect of the Final Solution, visited Finland in August 1942 and asked Prime Minister Jukka Rangell about the "Jewish Question", Rangell replied: "We do not have a Jewish Question." This culminated in a situation where Finnish Jewish soldiers fought beside the Nazis against the mutual Soviet threat.

The Jews even had their own field synagogue, and when Nazis found themselves outranked by a Jewish officer, they were forced to salute. As fellow combatants, some Jews were even awarded with an Iron Cross for bravery, which they understandably declined.

However, about ten refugees and twenty Jewish prisoners of war were finally handed over to Germany. They ended up in concentration camps or executed. Created in 1970 by artists Harry Kivijärvi and Sam Vanni, a memorial was built for them in Tähtitorninmäki, near the observatory.

To the West

RHODODENDRON PARK

A fantastic place in early summer

Paatsamatie 12
www.facebook.com/pages/Alppiruusupuisto/123953127687001
Open 24/7 — the best time to visit is usually late May to mid-June
Train station: Huopalahti station

There is no better place to visit in Helsinki in early summer than the Rhododendron Park in Etelä-Haaga, where the air is filled with the heady aroma of a million blooms. The ideal time to visit varies from year to year (find useful tips on the park's Facebook page), but is usually a couple of weeks during late May to mid-June. At other times the park is still pleasant to visit, with its overwhelming and soothing dense green foliage.

There are over 3,000 rhododendrons and many azaleas, most of them mighty bushes up to 5 metres in height. Elevated wooden passageways unique to this park offer a great view of the area. There are also benches available on the platforms and elsewhere, offering a fantastic opportunity to view the tops of the tall plants, which would otherwise be out of reach.

Power lines divide the park into two sections. In the older southern part you'll find most of the evergreen rhododendrons. The northern part was expanded in 1996 to include newer yellow rhododendrons and azaleas, closely related to other rhodos.

The park was founded in 1975 as an addition to the University of Helsinki's rhododendron breeding programme. The purpose of the programme was to find suitable species and varieties that could withstand the harsh Finnish winter, while offering different options in the growth of the bushes and the colours of the flowers.

Just over 50 years ago it was still deemed impossible to grow any rhododendrons in the latitudes of Finland, but successful breeding soon proved otherwise. Dozens of varieties bred in the park have been chosen for commercial production, a few of them named after their origins, such as "Helsinki University" and "Haaga". The parkland is unique on a global scale.

The only native rhododendrons to grow in Finland are wild rosemaries (suopursu, Rhododendron tomentosum), the extremely strong-smelling flower found in marshlands, and the rare arctic Rhododendron lapponicum (Lapland rosebay). Wild rosemary grows — you guessed it — wild on the borders of the parkland and offers an interesting sight on its own for foreign rhodo enthusiasts unfamiliar with this Nordic shrub.

STRÖMBERGINKOSKI WATERFALL ②

The only natural waterfall in the city

Tali Park area, south of Strömbergintie and north of Pitäjänmäki's industrial zone
Train: Pitäjänmäki station

In Finland's flat expanse, waterfalls are rare phenomena. Most of the more spectacular ones are located far from the capital, in the wilderness areas of Kainuu and Lapland.

However, an impressive example is the waterfall of Strömberginkoski in Pitäjänmäki, the only natural waterfall in the city. Though quite small, the water drops three metres over an almost vertical cliff. The rapids are part of Mätäjoki (Rotten river), a local stream fed by the swamps of Vantaa.

Right next to the fall is an atmospheric wooden bridge, from where you can watch the falls. You can also cross the river above the falls via the stepping stones set in the water. In winter the rapids become partially frozen and form a unique natural ice sculpture. The best times to visit the rapids are during periods of heavy rainfall and spring floods.

NEARBY
Pitäjänmäki cemetery ③

Sotarovastintie 7
Train: Mäkkylä station

Pitäjänmäki was an independent municipality during the Second World War. When the first casualties of the Winter War arrived, the locals decided to establish a military cemetery for them. A suitable spot was found and some 20 fallen soldiers were buried here. It was not until years later that a mistake was discovered: the sacred ground was actually on the side of Espoo, not Pitäjänmäki (or Helsinki). The mistake was corrected by annexing the area to the state of Finland, and the cemetery is now tended by the City of Helsinki.

Besides Pitäjänmäki, a number of other independent municipalities existed in the capital during the war, and their military cemeteries (or rather "hero cemeteries") can be found respectively from Munkkiniemi (Gert Skytte Park, at the corner of Ramsaynranta and Saunalahdentie), Lauttasaari (Myllykalliontie 1), Kulosaari, and Haaga (Sankaritie).

Unlike any other country in the world, Finland made a concerted effort to repatriate all of its fallen soldiers from the Second World War and bury each of them in their home city. The search for the missing continues even now. Since 1992 (after Russia allowed it), every year, volunteer workers on the old battlefields across the border in Russia find new bodies to repatriate. All of these cemeteries, large and small, were decorated with memorials, sculptures, crosses and so on. Every fallen soldier was buried in a similar grave, regardless of rank — equality and camaraderie was important.

MODEL OF THE SOLAR SYSTEM

Travel through the universe in a few hours

Patterimäki hill
Train: Pitäjänmäki station
From the station take the pedestrian tunnel south. The planets are on the highest parts of the hill, near the fortifications

The scale of the solar system, let alone the universe, is a hard thing to comprehend. Fortunately enough, in 1992 Tähtitieteellinen yhdistys URSA, the astronomical society of Finland, made things a little easier for visitors to Helsinki by building a scale model. It is located on the border of Helsinki and neighbouring Espoo, between Takkatie and Pajamäentie.

The scale is one to one billion, which still makes the dimensions of the model vast. The Sun, the centrepiece of any solar model, is located on the Pajamäki district's Patterimäki hill. It's on top of a 20-metre pole and measures some 1.4 metres in diameter. All planets are to scale, which means the nearest ones are very tiny, Mercury being just 4.9 mm. The only moons depicted in this model are our own and Pluto's minuscule moon, Kharon. Even though Pluto is not counted among the planets anymore, it is still part of the model for historical reasons.

The planets are made of metal and accompanied by informational signposts. The route can be easily covered in a few hours by bike, or you can choose to visit some of the inner planets on foot – Mercury to Saturn are within an easy 1.5 kilometres from the Sun, but Uranus, Neptune and Pluto are a little farther out. You can see the Sun even from the outer planets with binoculars. The route map and instructions can be found on URSA's website. This model makes an interesting excursion for all people fascinated by celestial matters.

Other scale models of the solar system in Europe

There are similar models on varying scales in several towns of Europe, including Goethenburg, Munich, York, Zagreb, La Couyère, Westerbork and Oxford. Some are so huge they are designed to be explored by car; some are built on smaller scales than the one in Helsinki. In the largest models the distance between the Sun to Pluto is around 300 kilometres, while in the smallest they are less than a kilometre apart.

BUNKER HILL

Forgotten relics of WWI Russian forts

The battlements are located around Patterimäki, between Pajamäentie and Takkatie/Arinatie in the north
Train: Pitäjänmäki station

Around Patterimäki (Bunker Hill) lies an impressive example of Russian First World War-era fortifications called "Krepost Sveaborg". This roughly semi-circular fortress complex of dozens of individual sites lurks on the borders of Helsinki.

Most of the complex that was not destroyed during the construction of the city is in bad shape, but in Pukinmäki the bunkers are easily recognisable. Some of the best preserved parts of Patterimäki are zig-zagging trenches, many over 2-metres-deep. There is also one remaining brick and mortar bunker on top of a small hill, along with more recent Second World War-era anti-aircraft bunkers.

In 1912, during the strain in international relations and the arms race that would eventually lead to World War I, Russia began planning a line of forts around the Grand Duchy's capital called "Krepost Sveaborg". It was one of the most important First World War fortifications in the world. Protecting the vital traffic hubs in Finland was part of a greater plan to protect St. Petersburg from a naval attack.

Most of the builders in Helsinki were Russian, but many unemployed Finns and Asian labourers also participated, creating a workforce that numbered 100,000 at its peak.

The fortress chain was built in a modern multi-polar style, with strongholds in hilltops (as many as 40 have been counted), bunkers, trenches and paved roads for the artillery to move around. Never completely finished, the last fortifications were made in February 1918, when the newly independent country was already collapsing into a bloody civil war. Some of the trenches and forts were actually used in the battles between the Whites and the Reds.

After independence, the fortified islands were still kept in military use, but most of the land fortifications were disarmed, stripped of useful equipment and abandoned. The ones that had steel reinforcements were destroyed in the interwar period and the steel sold as scrap.

Nowadays, the remaining parts of the fortress are hidden inside a landscape of quiet suburbs and busy ring roads, but it still gives a good impression of the fortification techniques of the time and is well worth a visit.

The renowned gay icon "Tom of Finland" (Touko Laaksonen), served here during the wars and became a decorated and respected war hero before leaving for America to become the famous creator of homoerotic art (see following page).

Tom of Finland: a decorated war hero

One of the most famous Finnish artists is undoubtedly Touko Laaksonen, better known as the icon of homoerotic art "Tom of Finland", a pioneer in his field. What is not widely known is that Laaksonen was also a decorated war hero, having served during the War of Continuation (1941–1944) in Helsinki's air defence, fighting against Soviet invaders.

When the Winter War broke out, Laaksonen was 19 years old. He'd had his matriculation exams the previous spring and was working in Turku as an assistant in a bookstore. He was drafted the following year.

The War of Continuation began in the summer of 1941. At the start of the war, Laaksonen served in air defence as an officer of a heavy anti-aircraft battery, and later as its head officer. He was promoted to lieutenant on 19 October 1943. In May of 1944 he was awarded the Cross of Liberty, one of the higher decorations in the Finnish military forces. According to his own testimony, the decoration was awarded for shooting down a Russian plane during the bombing of Helsinki.

Touko Laaksonen wasn't only an accomplished soldier, but also great at keeping up the morale of the troops. He went on tours, entertaining and singing with other soldiers, which helped keep up their spirits and prevented them falling into despair. On 21 September 1942 one of his performances was even broadcast on the radio.

The Soviet Union began the Karelian offensive against Finland on 9 June 1944. Helsinki was no longer the subject of bombings and Laaksonen's men were moved to Viipurinlahti, where he served until the end of the war. After returning home, Laaksonen moved permanently to Helsinki, where he began his studies at the Sibelius Academy and kick-started his world famous career.

SHORT ISLAND ARTWORK

An artwork that houses seabirds

Pikku Huopalahti
Tram: 8 — Munkkiniemen puistotie

Pikku Huopalahti is an elongated bay in the northwestern corner of the city. If you're here during the warm season, pay attention to the round platform-like island in the middle (best seen from the Munkkiniemi bridge).

This isle is actually a work of art built in 1997 by artist Kari Cavén on top of an old power-line post pedestal. Called *Lyhyt saari* (*Short Island*), its location and concept were chosen by the artist himself, who had been given free rein by the Helsinki Museum of Art.

After several sketches, Cavén chose this abandoned man-made isle and started building his artwork. It consisted of a steel frame, painted red then filled with soil and planted with mountain pines and grass. The vegetation was chosen to withstand harsh weather; it is the artist's wish that the island is not maintained in any way, so that all animals and plants can live here naturally on their own.

A few years after the artwork was created, the mountain pines had died and the island was sprouting mainly grass. However, it is still a cradle of new life. Seabirds, such as herring gulls, have made their home here and are raising their chicks on this formidable little sea fortress.

The antithesis of New York's Long Island

When asked why he named this artwork *Short Island*, Cavén declared it was the antithesis of New York's Long Island!

TWO STATUES OF YOUNG BOYS

Two statues forming a gateway

Gate of Munkkiniemi
Munkkiniemen puistotie 1 and 2

Munkkiniemen portti (Gate of Munkkiniemi) is a pair of buildings that forms a gateway. On each building, two small and easily missed statues of boys were made by the sculptor Mauno Oittinen in 1938. They are said to represent the sons of the real estate developer Martti Sorvari, called by their nicknames Jaska and Masa. One of them is about to throw a paper plane and the other is ready to catch it.

IRON AGE VILLAGE

A journey through time

Seurasaaren silta
Läntinen Pukkisaari island
From the middle of the bridge to Seurasaari, follow the trail west to Pukkisaaret
www.sommelo.fi

On the island of Läntinen Pukkisaari, take a turn to the right when crossing the bridge to Seurasaari; at the end of the short trail you'll find an enchanting Iron Age market village.

The village is maintained by a group called Sommelo, an ideological

association founded in 1997 with the purpose of furthering knowledge and research into the Finnish Prehistoric time, particularly the later Iron Age (550–1150/1300 Common Era). The group holds Iron Age markets and pagan weddings, activities for school groups, various courses and guided tours. It is always best check out their website for further information about future events, but the island and village are atmospheric to visit even when the market stalls are closed.

Läntinen Pukkisaari is a lot calmer than Seurasaari during the summer months, so it is worth considering if you want to enjoy a more private sunbathe or picnic. Just remember to take any trash away with you. On the opposite shore is the Tamminiemi Museum, the former home of long-time president Urho Kaleva Kekkonen.

POOR MAN STATUE

Charity for the deprived

Seurasaari Outdoor Museum
Seurasaarentie
02 9533 6912
seurasaari@kansallismuseo.fi
June—August, Monday—Sunday 11am—5pm; 15—31 May and 1—15
September, Monday—Friday 9am—3pm and Saturday—Sunday 11am—5pm
Bus: 24

In the bell tower of Karuna Church, within Seurasaari Outdoor Museum, is a curious statue of a man, smartly dressed in suit and top hat. This statue was acquired by the museum from Haapavesi in 1912. The ragged hole in the statue's chest was caused by robbers who broke into the money box inside it — there used to be a protective iron panel with a hole for the coins.

The statue is one of the few remaining examples in Helsinki of the so-called "poor man statues" (*vaivaisukko* in Finnish), carved, human-shaped alms boxes that represent poor and disabled men begging. Their origins date back to 1649 when Queen Christina gave an order to distribute "poor logs" to churches and other public places. Soon these were modified to look like beggars. Donations were collected by parishes and channelled to help the poor and disabled. This was especially important after the Finnish War (1808–1809), as the amount of widows, orphans and disabled veterans was high. Many of the statues were specifically made to resemble a retired soldier from the Finnish War, sporting army uniforms and missing a limb. Most of them have a money box inside and a coin slot. There is often a biblical sentence written above.

Across the country there are statues of 144 poor men and one poor woman, many still in their original places outside churches. Most of the Finnish statues are found in Ostrobothnia, one theory being that their sculptors were the same carpenters who made wooden figureheads in this area, strong in shipbuilding.

Built in 1685 in Sauvo, the wooden Karuna Church was transferred to Seurasaari in 1912 in order to be included in the museum's collection of traditional Finnish architecture. The church remains one of the city's most popular places for weddings. The paintings and arm-shaped chandeliers originate from Germany and may be spoils from the Thirty Years' War (1618–1648). Many treasures were looted during this conflict, which brought the Finnish *Hakkapeliittas* to lasting fame as part of the Swedish army. These light cavalryman were known as fierce warriors, riding the ancestors of the modern-day Finnish horse, a native breed. *Hakkapeliitta* is a modification of a contemporary name given by their enemies in Holy Roman Empire, variously spelled as *Hackapelite*, *Hackapell*. These terms were based on their battle cry "hakkaa päälle", commonly translated as "Cut them down!"

THE GRAVE WITH THE CANNONBALL

The almost unknown soldier of Lauttasaari

Länsiväylä highway at the corner of Taivaanvuohentie and Pohjoiskaari
Metro : Lauttasaari

Just by the side of the Länsiväylä highway, at the corner of Taivaan-vuohentie and Pohjoiskaari, a door in a sound barrier fence allows access to a large stone, embedded in which is an iron cannonball. This is the grave of a soldier who died in the Crimean War (1853–1857) while defending Lauttasaari.

During the bombardment of Viapori in 1855, two frigates and one corvette began firing upon Lauttasaari. The fleet tried twice to land, but both times the counterfire from Lauttasaari was so intense that the invaders had to fall back. During the second landing attempt, however, one soldier from a grenadier-sniper battalion in Lauttasaari was killed. He was buried under a large natural stone with a mounted cannonball bearing the text (in Swedish): "Fell defending this island in Särkiniemi 9.8.1855, peace be upon his dust." Although the grave is still known as the "grave of the unknown soldier", his identity was in fact discovered in 1958: Joseph Johan Back, from Närpiö.

There is another lesser-known grave of an English soldier of the Crimean War in Isosaari (see page 245).

Oolannin sota (War of Åland)

The Crimean War was fought between October 1853 and March 1856 between Imperial Russia and an alliance of French, British, Ottoman and Sardinian troops. Motivated by Russian expansionism, the war ended with the defeat of Russia. Even though the war is generally known as the Crimean War, battles were fought all across Eastern Europe, from the Baltic to the Caucasus, with some campaigns even in the Russian Far East.

In Finland the war is also known as *Oolannin sota* (War of Åland), because much of the fighting took place in Åland and, to a lesser extent, other parts of Finland. Sometimes *Oolannin sota* is used to mean the entire Crimean War, sometimes only the battles that took place in Åland.

There's a famous Finnish song from the 1850s about *Oolannin sota* known as *Oolannin sota oli kauhia* ("War of Åland was terrible"). Researchers Jerker Örjans and Pirjo Liisa-Niinimäki discovered a few years ago that the song was probably written by Finnish soldiers taken by the English as prisoners of war.

NEARBY
Anti-aircraft gun ⑪

At the highest point of Myllykallio Hill stands an original 76 mm anti-aircraft gun, affectionately called "Itko", that was used in the city's air defence during the so-called Great Raids Against Helsinki (Helsingin suurpommitukset). A plaque reminds visitors that over 20,000 bombs were dropped on Helsinki by Soviet planes. Due to the activities of Helsinki's air defence, only 800 of them hit their target. Myllykallio hosted an anti-aircraft battery in 1939-1940 during the Winter War and again in 1941-1944 during the War of Continuation.

SISÄ-HATTU ISLAND

Walk this way

Access from Ryssänkärki beach (buses 65A and 66A from city centre)
Access from the southern shore of Lauttasaari, Lauttasaaren ulkoilupuisto
(walk across the sea to the island)

In Lauttasaari, Sisä-Hattu (The Inner Hat) is a small and secret uninhabited island. The island can easily be seen, but most people don't know that even if the water looks deep (and it is deep on both sides of the path), an underwater stone path offers safe access. Even if the path is completely submerged in water, you should still be able to walk across.

The easiest way to get there is to walk from Ryssänkärki beach: as you look towards the sea, walk to the left and you'll find a small path that leads to the island.

Though the island has had no permanent settlement in modern times, it has, nevertheless, had its share of visitors over the years. The area is filled with stone carvings, some dating from the Russian period. There are also rocks with poems carved in Swedish, carvings of strange symbols and old coats-of-arms. One peculiar carving is of a compass that shows the direction you are facing when on Sisä-Hattu.

SMALL ELEPHANT CARVINGS

The remains of an art exhibit in 2007

At the end of Särkiniementie in Särkiniemen puisto
Metro: Lauttasaari

The little southwestern peninsula of Särkiniemi in Lauttasaari leaves many visitors puzzled. What do the small elephants carved here and there on the smooth cliffs mean?

In 2007, the LaruArt art exhibit invited German artist Patrick Timm to do an environmental piece for the Lauttasaari island. He chose to carve these tiny animals to decorate the Ice Age coastal rock formations.

Some environmentalists have been angered by this; they felt the cliffs were good enough in their natural state and that the carvings didn't add anything to them.

Carving names and figures has been a common habit among Finnish people for centuries. Among the most famous are the Hauensuoli rock carvings near Hanko, now on the tentative list of Unesco World Heritage sites. The island of Gaddtarmen (Hauensuoli) off Hango (Hanko) forms a natural harbour on a sailing route in the east-west direction. Sailors have made more than 400 carvings on the rocks while awaiting favourable winds. The oldest drawings date from the 15th and 16th centuries. Most of the carvings depict coats-of-arms of Swedish and Finnish gentry.

Other lesser-known carvings dot the coastline, ranging from ancient to modern texts and pictures. See also page 218 (Kruunuvuori) and page 144 (Sisä-Hattu).

PAAVO NURMI SCULPTURE

A fantastic student joke

Polyteekkarimuseo
Otaniemi Campus
Jämeräntaival 3 A – 02150 Espoo
For tour inquiries: museo@ayy.fi – www.polyteekkarimuseo.fi

Located in the heart of Otaniemi Campus, Polyteekkarimuseo is one of the few museums in Finland focused on student culture, namely the lively community of students of technology, or *teekkari*. Although it showcases their history in documents and artefacts, such as their signature boilersuits (*haalarit*) and tasseled student caps, the most remarkable artefact is a small statue of runner Paavo Nurmi.

A miniature of the well-known statue found outside the Olympic Stadium in Helsinki, it was the centrepiece of a joke carefully planned by four students.

Teekkari students are known for their particular humour and practical jokes (*jäynä*). On their way to a Vappu student fest in Gothenburg (1 May 1961), when the 17th century battleship Vasa was put into its present museum in Stockholm, the Finnish students managed to hide the statue of Nurmi on the ship's deck during the night-time; one of them (a journalist for a student newspaper) had a press pass granting him special access. The Swedish marine archaeologists were puzzled. It took them a whole day to realise it was not the statue of some ancient deity, but a contemporary Finnish athlete.

The students had chosen the legendary middle- and long-distance runner Paavo Nurmi as a centrepiece because of his place in sporting history: Nurmi was dubbed "The Flying Finn", and was a winner of nine gold and three silver Olympic medals. His career and his participation in the 1932 Los Angeles Summer Olympics was marred by accusations of professionalism (supposedly forbidden for Olympic athletes until 1988) made by some Swedish sportspeople. This had rendered the two countries' already competitive sporting relationship strained for decades. Nurmi retired from running and became a coach for the Finnish national team. He was also given the honour of lighting the Olympic fire at the 1952 Helsinki Summer Olympics.

VILLA GYLLENBERG

A very charming little-known museum

Kuusisaarenpolku 11
www.gyllenbergs.fi
Wednesday 4pm—8pm, Sunday 12pm—4pm or by request
Closed in July

Formerly the home of Signe and Ane Gyllenberg, Villa Gyllenberg is a very charming little-known museum that now houses their remarkable art collection.

The pale orange villa dates from 1938 and was expanded in 1955; the Gyllenbergs wanted very early on to open their art treasures to the public. After the connoisseur couple passed away, the family home was opened as a museum in 1980.

Commercial counsellor Ane Gyllenberg had a profound relationship with art. He was an active Freemason and later became the grand master of his lodge. He was also a supporter of the esoteric anthroposophy movement of Rudolf Steiner (1861–1925): true to the anthroposophic principles, Ane Gyllenberg considered art to be a tool for inner development and spiritual growth. His personal favourites were often portraits of people from different walks of life, which is apparent when viewing the collection.

Aside from art by Finnish painters and Old Masters, the collection includes rare musical instruments, such as the 1732 Bergonzi violin. The violin was built in Cremona, Italy, by Carlo Bergonzi (1683–1747), a student of the famous craftsman Antonio Stradivari. The precious violin is occasionally loaned to outstanding Finnish violinists for a period of three years.

The museum's collection is growing all the time, and the exhibition is arranged chronologically. Parts of the museum are maintained as they were during the Gyllenberg's time and retain the atmosphere of bourgeoisie domestic bliss. Villa Gyllenberg also has a pleasant café with views of the Laajalahti bay.

The most famous painting in this museum is *Ad Astra*, an intriguing symbolist work by Akseli Gallén-Kallela. The  painting dates from 1894 and features a striking image of a young woman with arms raised, naked and standing in the water, framed by the full moon and her own fiery hair. A very special painting for the artist, it was used as an altarpiece in the baptisms of his children. Gallén-Kallela never sold the original version, considering it to be a sort of artistic manifesto. He claimed it was about Resurrection and the Saviour; the girl in the picture has stigmata, which he painted over in another version of the painting.

The name "ad astra" means "towards the stars" in Latin, from the proverb "per aspera ad astra", which means "through hardships to the stars".

FUTURO HOUSE

A movable ski cabin

WeeGee exhibition centre
Ahertajantie 5
May–early September Tuesday–Thursday 11am–6pm, Wednesday–Friday
11am–7pm, Saturday–Sunday 11am–5pm
Metro: Tapiola

The WeeGee Exhibition Centre in Tapiolain hosts some fascinating exhibits: the Espoo Museum of Modern Art, Espoo City Museum, Hevosenkenkä Toy Museum and the Clock Museum. But one of the most interesting exhibits is the 1968 plastic Futuro House in the courtyard.

This elliptic building looks like a stereotypical flying saucer and is commonly known as the "UFO house" – it even has an airplane-like hatch. With the serial number 001, it is one of only 65 in existence in the world, and one of just two on public display (the prototype, number 000, is in Baijmans Van Beuningen Museum in Rotterdam). The house was owned by Matti Kuusla in rustic Hirvensalmi between 1968 and 2011 before it was donated to the museum.

Futuro is a prefabricated plastic house designed by architect Matti Suuronen that manifests the futuristic, space-age aspirations of the 1960s. The utopian house was originally intended for use in remote Alpine environments as a movable ski cabin. The only requirements for its placement were four small concrete pillars, so it could be attached to almost any topography.

Though it gained global fame at the time, it proved too exotic and expensive for the mass market. The oil crisis of 1973 tripled the price of plastic and finally crushed all dreams of launching Futuro on a large scale.

The WeeGee Exhibition Centre is housed in an old printing house, of which some vestiges remain: the load-bearing structures, some of the old façades, offices at the north-eastern end, one of the printing rooms, and round emergency exit stairs.

THE FRESCOES OF ESPOO CATHEDRAL

Intriguing little-known frescoes

Kirkkopuisto 5
Espoo
09 8050 3600
September–May, Tuesday–Friday 10am–5pm, Saturday–Sunday
10am–6pm; June–August, daily 10am–6pm, Monday–Sunday 11am–5pm

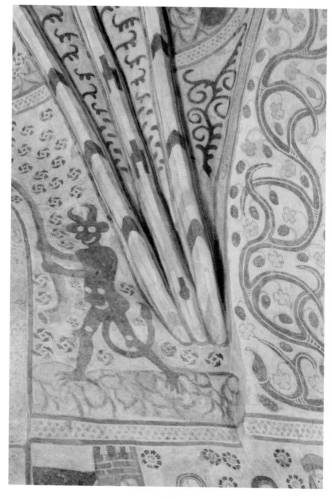

Espoo Cathedral is one of two medieval stone churches in the region (along with the Church of St. Lawrence) dedicated to Matthew the Apostle (Matteus) and considered to be the most important historic building in Espoo. A consecration cross next to the main entrance was painted after the cathedral was finished in the 1480s. Only parts of the medieval walls remain, but the rich frescoes make the visit worthwhile. Considered ugly and superstitious during Protestant times, they were painted over with white chalk. Fortunately, the paintings survived and have been revealed in a process that began in 1931.

On the western side of the main nave's fourth cupola, two devils are pulling a pig's skin between them: this scene is from the Finnish folktale about the Devil writing down the names of people gossiping during the service. In a popular version of the tale, only the truly pious man has the special power to see the Devil, who is stretching the skin in order to fit more names on it. The Devil stretches the skin so much he falls over. The pious man laughs and the Devil proceeds to write down his name for laughing during service. Now turned sinner, the pious man loses sight of the Devil.

In the first cupola of the southern nave, another fresco depicts a pelican feeding her young with her own blood, a symbol adopted by early Christians to symbolise Christ.

The eastern part of the northern nave has another fresco showing witches riding to Kyöpelinvuori (Blåkulla): according to legend, this mountain was where the witches feasted and fornicated with the Devil during Easter. The witches were thought to either fly or ride there using unorthodox vehicles such as broomsticks, calves and mattocks.

Other details (ask the church guide to point them out) can be found on the tiles of the central column supporting the roof. A medieval rooster stepped on the wet brick and left his footprint there; there are also a child's toe prints and a dog's paw mark.

Next to the church is a memorial to those buried in the areas that Finland lost to the Soviet Union in the Second World War.

NUUKSIO ORBICULAR ROCK

A natural wonder

Nuuksio National Park
Haukkalammentie
Espoo
The rock is on the northeastern side of the crossroads, where the asphalt road turns into Haukkalampi. It can be found using Google Maps

Though many people visit the Nuuksio National Park in the summer months, most of them miss the Nuuksio Orbicular Rock (Koivulan pallokivi), a true geological wonder.

Discovered in the 1920s, this rare variety of magmatic rock is internationally famous among geologists. The rock bed is a few hundred metres long and has a couple of outcrops where the orbs are visible. It is advisable to take a water bottle with you when you visit the rock; the orbs are much clearer when you pour water on them.

The typical features of orbicular rocks are round bodies, called "orbicules", which vary in size and composition. They are probably formed through nucleation around a grain in cooling magma. They can be found in only a few hundred locations in the world.

The Nuuksio National Park was established in 1994 with the residents of Helsinki and nearby metropolitan areas in mind. Comprising the western park of Nuuksio lake highlands, the park is covered by dense forest and numerous bodies of water. It is a barren environment, which has so far saved it from being cut down for agriculture. The high cliffs offer beautiful views of the park and its lakes.

The little marshy "islands" on Mustalampi Lake (featured on several marked trails) are the result of the rising water levels in the 1950s. Nearby swamps were flooded and these areas have floated on the surface ever since, giving the local waterfowl a safe nesting place.

The name Nuuksio (Noux in Swedish) comes from the Sami language — "njukca" meaning "swan". The nomadic Sami roamed these woods in medieval times, but were driven to northern Lapland long ago.

The cute, wide-eyed Siberian Flying Squirrel is the symbol of the national park. This species can be seen on the very western fringes of Nuuksio, most of them residing in Asiatic forests as the name suggests.

To the North-East

THE SWASTIKA ON THE HANSA PLANE AT THE AVIATION MUSEUM

The oldest aircraft built in Finland, not at all a Nazi plane

Tietotie 3 — Vantaa
09 8700870
info@suomenilmailumuseo.fi
Monday—Tuesday and Thursday—Sunday, 10am—5pm; Wednesday 10am—8pm
Train: Aviapolis station

Sited near the Helsinki-Vantaa airport, the Aviation Museum (Ilmailumuseo) hosts a very special aircraft, emblazoned with the swastika symbol. Surprisingly enough, this plane is not a Nazi fighter, but the oldest aircraft ever built in Finland.

Dating from 1922, the design of this plane is based on a German Hansa-Brandenburg seaplane. It was built in the Air Force's factory in the dry dockyard of Suomenlinna, which had been in operation since 1920. Hansa seaplanes were used until 1935.

The first motorised flight in Finland was performed in 1911, and the Finnish Air Force was established in 1918 during the Civil War.

Founded in 1977 and based on a collection of airplanes that had been on display (with detached wings) in the Helsinki-Vantaa airport corridors since 1972, the museum has two huge halls that hold a collection of 82 different civilian and military aircraft.

The swastika is the old symbol of the Finnish air forces, dating from the Civil War. It is still in use by the Finnish Air Force.

The swastika: a symbol that predates the Nazis

The swastika, a sacred symbol for thousands of years, is found in many ancient civilisations: among the Celts and Etruscans, in Northern Europe, Central America (Maya) and North America (Navajo Indians), and in Asia (mainly China, Tibet and India). Some believe Tibet was the true origin of the symbol: the cross would simply be "drawn" on the slopes of the mythical Mount Kailash in western Tibet, sacred to Hindus and Buddhists and thought to be the source of the world's energy.

It is important to distinguish between swástika and sowástika (in Pali and Tibetan) – in Western languages, swastika and sauvastika. The sauvastika cross rotates to the left and is considered sinister and regressive by Eastern religions and the peoples of Western antiquity, who considered the swastika rotating to the right a benevolent and evolutionary symbol. Adolf Hitler and his peers appropriated this symbol, making it the evil sauvastika.

Thus the direction of rotation of the swastika or sauvastika determines its astronomical and cosmic significance: in a clockwise direction, positive, solar, it symbolises Universal Evolution and is typified by the swastika adopted by Charlemagne. In an anti-clockwise direction, negative, lunar, it indicates Planetary Involution and the intention of subjecting the timeless and sacred to the strictly temporal and profane space, as typified by the sauvastika adopted by Hitler. Because of the arms of the cross (crux gammata, after the Greek letter gamma), branches that leave behind a fiery trail as they turn, the swastika is the symbol of Universal Action. In this sense, it has always accompanied the graphic, pictorial or carved image of the saviours of humanity, the messiahs, or avatars such as Christ. Christ is depicted in the ancient Roman catacombs at the centre of a spiral-shaped swastika because he represents the Spiritual Centre or Pole where the Supreme God resides, who gave rise to the gods, mankind and other living beings. It is the symbol of the Creator, around which are arranged hierarchies of beings emanating from his unique Centre (Bindu, Sanskrit for "point" or "dot"). Like Christ, the Anointed One, who is the Mystical Centre of Christianity, Buddha, the Enlightened One, marks the Mystical Pole of the Buddhist faith, indicated in mankind through the Heart, the expression of spiritual consciousness – sufficient reason for many images of Buddha to have a swastika engraved on the chest.

A GOOD SOLDIER OR A TRAITOR ②

A cursed tomb?

The tomb of Carl Olof Cronstedt
Kirkkotie 45
09 8306224 – tikkurilan.seurakunta@evl.fi
Summer Monday–Friday 9am–8pm; winter Monday–Friday 9am–3pm
Bus: 633 – Isopelto

Built around 1450, Pyhän Laurin kirkko (The Church of Saint Lawrence) is the oldest remaining building in the capital area. The church was restored after suffering heavy fire damage in 1893. In the old graveyard around the church, there is a small burial chapel for Carl Olof

Cronstedt and his wife Beata Sofia Wrangel; it is said to be cursed.

Cronstedt had a distinguished military career, having even served in the British Royal Navy in 1776-1779; he took part in the American Revolutionary War, spending a long time as a prisoner of war. While serving in the Swedish Navy, he also beat the Russian forces in the Battle of Svensksund in 1790, the largest naval battle ever fought in the Baltic Sea.

Cronstedt was a controversial figure in Finnish history, serving as a vice-admiral in the Swedish Navy during the Finnish War (1808–1809). Some thought of him as a good soldier, others considered him a traitor. In the epic Finnish poem *The Tales of Ensign Stål* it's even suggested that Cronstedt sold Viapori castle to the Russians, but historians doubt this. After the war, Cronstedt was sentenced to death for high treason in absentia, but was later pardoned by Alexander I of Russia. Cronstedt lived the rest of his life in Herttoniemi mansion. He died in 1820 and was buried in the private burial chapel in Pyhän Laurin kirkko's cemetery.

According to legend, strange things happened during the burial of the vice-admiral: immediately after Cronstedt's body was placed in the chapel, vipers crawled out of the ground to prevent access. People tried to kill them, but more appeared. As a last resort, they carved at the entrance a symbol of Ouroboros — a snake biting its own tail, and the abstract representation of eternity (see following double page). The vipers left, and when Cronstedt's wife was buried in the chapel a few years later, no vipers showed up.

The Ouroboros: a symbol of divine illumination

The figure of a coiled serpent biting its own tail is sometimes found in iconography and literature. This symbol is traditionally known as the *Ouroboros* or *Uroboros*, a Greek word derived from the Coptic and Hebrew languages – *ouro* is Coptic for "king" and *ob* Hebrew for "serpent" – meaning "royal serpent". Thus the reptile raising its head above its body is used as a symbol of mystical illumination: for Eastern peoples, it represents the divine fire they call Kundalini. Kundalini is the origin of the association that Western medicine of the Middle Ages and Renaissance made between, on the one hand, the body heat that rises from the base of the spine to the top of the head and, on the other, the *venena bibas* ("ingested venom" mentioned by Saint Benedict of Nursia) of the snake whose bite can only be treated by an equally potent poison. Just as the Eastern techniques of spiritual awakening, Dzogchen and Mahamudra, show how a meditating person must learn to "bite his tail like the serpent", the theme of the *Ouroboros* and ingested venom is a reminder that spiritual awareness can only result from a devout life: by elevating your consciousness onto a mental plane surpassing the ordinary, you search within to truly find yourself as an eternal being. The Greeks popularised the word ouroboros in its literal sense of "serpent biting its tail". They acquired this image from the Phoenicians through contact with the Hebrews, who had themselves adopted it from Egypt where the Ouroboros featured on a stele dated as early as 1600 BC. There it represented the sun god Ra (Light), who resurrects life from the darkness of the night (synonymous with death), going back to the theme of eternal return, life, death, and the renewal of existence, as well as the reincarnation of souls in successive human bodies until they have reached their evolutionary peak, which will leave them perfect, both physically and spiritually – a theme dear to Eastern peoples.

In this sense, the serpent swallowing itself can also be interpreted as an interruption of the cycle of human development (represented by the serpent) in order to enter the cycle of spiritual evolution (represented by the circle).

Pythagoras associated the serpent with the mathematical concept of infinity, coiled up as zero – the abstract number used to denote eternity, which becomes reality when the *Ouroboros* is depicted turning around on itself.

Gnostic Christians identified it with the Holy Spirit revealed through wisdom to be the Creator of all things visible and invisible, and whose ultimate expression on Earth is Christ. For this reason, the symbol is associated in Greek Gnostic literature with the phrase *hen to pan* (The All is One); it was commonly adopted in the 4th and 5th centuries as a protective amulet against evil spirits and venomous snakebites. This amulet was known as Abraxas, the name of a god in the original Gnostic pantheon that the Egyptians recognised as Serapis. It became one of the most famous magical talismans of the Middle Ages.

Greek alchemists very quickly espoused the figure of the *Ouroboros* and so it reached the Hermetic philosophers of Alexandria – among them, Arab thinkers who studied and disseminated this image in their schools of Hermeticism and alchemy.

These schools were known and sought out by medieval Christians. There is even historical evidence that members of the Order of the Knights Templar, as well as other Christian mystics, travelled to Cairo, Syria and even Jerusalem to be initiated into the Hermetic sciences.

STONE AND MINERAL PARK NEAR HEUREKA SCIENCE CENTRE

A permanent bedrock exhibition

Kuninkaalantie 7 – Vantaa
Free entry
Train: Tikkurila station

As you approach Heureka Science Centre in Tikkurila, Vantaa, you'll notice a large field full of boulders. Seldom explored in detail by the science enthusiasts and children rushing into the building, it offers an interesting overview of the literal foundations of Finland – this area is a permanent bedrock exhibition, containing both common and rare types of rocks found in Finland.

The boulders are situated to reflect their distribution throughout different geographical provinces of the country. The 124 rocks vary from Ordovician limestone (from the Åland islands) to gold ore (from Lapland) and several volcanic rocks and semiprecious stones from around the country, highlighting the variation within Finland's vast and ancient geology.

There are also parts of the rocky, raised coastline from Vantaa, formed on the shores of the Baltic after the Ice Age. Other curiosities include the oldest signs of life in Finland, a 2100 million-year-old stromatolite,

and ancient ocean ripple marks on a stone from Tervola.

Near the main entrance, visitors are greeted by perennial gardens that were planted in accordance with the historical classification system designed by Carolus Linnaeus.

Heureka Science Centre was opened in 1989 and has since showcased physics, chemistry, archaeology, linguistics, astronomy and other branches of science in various interactive ways.

VANTAA GERMAN MILITARY CEMETERY

A lonely monument among the roadside bushes

Siltaniitynkuja 3
Vantaa

Over 200,000 German soldiers served in Finland in the War of Continuation (1941–1944) and over 15,000 of them fell. Most of them were buried in makeshift cemeteries beyond the borders of modern Finland, with no grave marker other than a wooden stick or cross. Nazis had plans to gather the skeletons and place them in grand ossuaries, but their plans were ruined in their defeat.

Post-war West Germany began collecting all the bodies it could. Part of this project were two cemeteries established in the 1950s for soldiers buried on Finnish soil, from where they would be exhumed and reburied: the larger of the two is near Rovaniemi, Lapland; the smaller one in Vantaa has 364 soldiers from the southern battlefields along with six German soldiers from the First World War (Finnish Civil War).

The cemetery is squeezed between the old and new highways to Lahti and the modern Vantaa prison complex. It was originally approached through an entrance hall and a fence of natural stone that was constructed by a group of German youngsters in the 1950s as a summer job. The graves were located in small groups.

The cemetery was originally connected to the nearby Honkanummi Cemetery, but in 1973 the highway isolated it. You can still see the barred gate of the abandoned entrance from the highway, a lonely monument among the roadside bushes – a statue of two figures embracing, along with engraved biblical verses in German. The new, less grandiose entrance is from the old highway.

Beneath the circular pavement lies a mass grave for 200 sailors whose bodies were recovered from Finnish waters after two German warships ran into their own mines on 12 December 1944; over 400 others were never found.

It was often impossible to correctly identify the skeletons so many are buried together and marked by a single headstone stating, for example, "Zwei Deutsche Soldaten" – also a common practise in German military cemeteries on the Western Front.

AARNIPATA AND RAUNINMALJA GIANT'S KETTLES

Among the oldest giant's kettles in the world

Corner of Rapakiventie and Lucina Hagmanin polku
Train: Pihlajamäki station

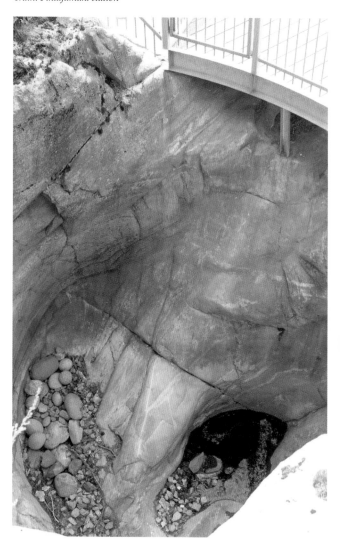

At the corner of Rapakiventie and Lucina Hagmanin polku, a fenced area contains two eight metre-deep gigantic holes. These two giant's kettles (*hiidenkirnu* in Finnish) are called Aarnipata and Rauninmalja. Their names are references to Finnish folklore and the result of a competition held in 2008.

Aarnipata is one of the biggest giant's kettles in Finland, over 7 metres in diameter and 8 metres deep. The two kettles still contain their pebbles, which once ground out the holes in the swirls of a glacial stream. It feels strange to call them pebbles, as the biggest one is over 1.6 metres in diameter and weighs 6 tons.

Giant's kettles are very common in Finland; there are over 10,000 examples, most lying undiscovered beneath loose soil. Many were born during the thaw of the last glacial period, known as Weichselian glaciation, some 10,000 years ago. However, the two kettles in Pihlajanmäki are very special; they date from 50,000–70,000 years ago and are among the oldest giant's kettles in the world.

The kettles were discovered in 1993 during construction work. The story says the explosives were set to blast the rock away, when geology enthusiast Sulo Savolainen spotted them and cancelled the deed just moments before detonation.

What is a giant's kettle?

Glacial potholes, or giant's kettles (*hiidenkirnu* in Finnish) are cavities or holes that have been drilled into the rock by eddying currents of water bearing stones. In old times they were thought to be of supernatural origin and work as cooking pots for the demon folk (*hiisi* = a goblin, *kirnu* = churn).

There is a third, smaller kettle in Pihlajamäki, from the Weichselian period, between Johtokivenkuja and Johtokiventie streets, on the little cliff behind the block houses. Another pair of giant's kettles can be found in Roihuvuori, in the forest east of Punahilkantie.

THE GRAVE OF POLICE DOG LEX ⑥

A dog that managed to catch 108 criminals alone

Metsäläntie
Plot A-455
09 5420 0100
Open 24/7
Bus: From Elielinaukio — Metsäläntie

In the central park on the south side of Metsäläntie, the largest pet cemetery in Finland, created in 1947, is the final resting place of several famous Finnish animals, including the beloved dog of President Juho Kusti Paasikivi, and Pörri, the war dog who protected Finland in the Second World War. It is also the location of a memorial to the millions of animals that have died in medical experiments so that we humans could live a healthier, more secure life.

Although there are about 3,000 animals buried in the cemetery, one of its occupants holds a special place among the legends. Lex was an extremely famous police dog, and one of the first of his kind in Finland. He was a big, handsome German Shepherd, known for his unmatched prowess in the line of canine police work. He fought unrelentingly for justice with his owner Veikko Ylönen, who was one of the pioneering figures in the introduction of police dogs to Finland.

In his lifetime, Lex managed to catch 108 criminals, alone. If you count the arrests he made with his owner, the figure rises to several hundreds. Lex's fame soared as he took down several higher profile cases, and the criminal underworld began to fear him. Several criminals vowed to kill Lex. And several tried. One of the most famous of these was the notorious bank robber Matti "Volvo" Markkanen, who tried to shoot Lex at point blank range ... but missed. The noise from the gun caused damage to Lex's ear and nervous system. Markkanen managed to escape, becoming one of the few to ever do so. And Lex had to take his only day off from work.

In 1975 Lex finally met his match. He and his partner were hunting burglars in Espoo. When the burglars noticed Lex, they set a trap and ambushed him, shooting the dog five times. Lex didn't die immediately; even in his death throes he had the strength to return to his owner, giving Veikko one final lick of appreciation before collapsing and passing away. Lex's death was a day of sorrow for the entire Finnish police force.

RAUHANASEMA BUILDING ⑦

An old railway station transported from the Karelian Isthmus

Veturitori 3
Train: Pasila station

Seemingly out of place among the gritty beton brutalist surroundings of Eastern Pasila, Rauhanasema (Peace station) is an old wooden neoclassical building that was originally a railway station house. Built in 1915, it comes from Vammeljoki, a town in the Karelian Isthmus, an area that Finland lost to the Soviet Union in the Second World War. The railway station had been the local headquarters of the Reds during the Finnish Civil War, because the town hall was deemed too small.

After Finnish independence, traffic on the coastal railway near the border had almost died out and the station was left without a purpose. In 1923 it was moved to Pasila, log by log, to serve as the local railway station.

In 1984 the modern and huge Pasila railway station was built and the old station house was moved again, this time some one hundred metres to the east. The building was renovated by volunteers and opened under its new name "Rauhanasema" in 1986. Nowadays, the building hosts various non-governmental organisations.

Other old wooden railway stations in Helsinki
Pitäjänmäki: built 1904
Oulunkylä: built 1922
Malmi: built 1934
Huopalahti: built 1906
Tapanila: dismantled and moved to Huopalahti
Käpylä: pulled down in the 1970s
Pukinmäki: pulled down in 2010
Puistola: pulled down in 2001

SITE OF THE FIRST CHURCH IN HELSINKI

Humble foundations of the future capital

Koskelantie 43
At the end of Vanhankaupungintie
Bus: Tekniikan Museo

In Kirkkorinne, in an area known today as Kustaa Vaasa's Park, a sandy area fenced by stones in the middle of the park marks the foundations of the first church to be established in Helsinki. An old tombstone indicates the location of the church entrance and a sign tells of the origins of the city.

Helsinki was founded in 1550 by King Gustav I of the prestigious Vasa family of Sweden. The first time the church is mentioned in any writings is in 1553 when the local parish asked for money from the king to build a new church.

Built in wood, the first church had an earthen floor and only acquired pews after 1600. The foundations were built from natural rocks, which are the only remaining part of the church. The church was in use until 1670, when it was destroyed either by natural decay or by fire.

In 1866 pieces of an old headstone were found in the ruins of the church. They belonged to the tomb of Hans van Sanden, one of the few people from 16th century Helsinki still known today. He was a merchant and a burgher, probably of Dutch origin and later immortalised in the historical novels of writer Ursula Pohjolan-Pirhonen. In 1890 the sculptor Robert Stigell created a replica of the original tombstone, which was placed on the site of the first church. The tombstone has the coat-of-arms of Jägerhorn, the family of Hans van Sanden's wife Anna Henrikintytär Jägerhorn.

The tombstone includes a small mistake: it claims that Hans van Sanden died in 1590, even though the church books claim that he was still alive in the year 1594.

KUUSILUOTO ISLAND

An island inhabited only by sheep

Kuusiluoto island
Bus: 78 — Koskelan varikko
Take the trail from the bridge at the mouth of river Vantaanjoki, which will turn into a wooden elevated pathway at the seaside. About 700 metres later you'll reach Lammassaari, which you must cross to enter Kuusiluoto

Among the many Helsinki area islands, Kuusiluoto, part of the Van-hankaupunginlahti-Viikki nature reserve, is pretty unique in that it is inhabited only by sheep. Surprisingly, Lammassaari (The Sheep Isle), its neighbouring island, has no sheep, despite its name. In 1905 a Finnish temperance society called Koitto (Dawn) rented Lammassaari to provide houses for its members. Since then, sheep have gradually relocated to Kuusiluoto. Lammassaari is a conservation area, home to a wide array of different bird species and all kinds of mammals, including moose.

Kuusiluoto can be accessed via a duckboard trail that leads through Lammassaari. A fence runs all around the island and one should close all the gates when moving in and out of Kuusiluoto so that the sheep won't get away. A walk around Kuusiluoto and Lammassaari takes about two hours.

You can get to Lammassaari and Kuusiluoto by walking from a track leaving from Matinsilta bridge at the mouth of Vantaanjoki. The track leads to a bridge that crosses the sea to Lammassaari through a large reed bed occupied by many bird species. There's a path of duckboards leading around the island. On the eastern coast, a birdwatching tower offers a great view of the Viikki bay. Atop the highest part of Lammassaari is Pohjolan pirtti, an old timber log house from 1905.

STATUE OF CATHERINE OF SAXE-LAUENBURG

The naked queen

Verkatehtaanpuisto
Near the Vanhankaupunginkoski stream pool

In Vanhankaupunki, on a rocky outcrop of the park near the foundation site of Helsinki, a statue of a naked lady has sat since 2014. Surprisingly, this unusual work by artist Hannu Tapani Konttinen depicts the Swedish queen Catherine of Saxe-Lauenburg (1513-1535). The statue is still very little known, except to the locals jogging by.

According to official history, Catherine was often presented as a bad example, in contrast to Gustav's second queen, Margaret Leijonhufvud. Is this the reason why she is represented naked?

Queen of Sweden between 1531 and 1535, Catherine was the first wife of King Gustav I, and mother to the infamous Eric XIV. Born in Ratzeburg (Germany) to Magnus I, Duke of Saxe-Lauenburg, her marriage to Gustav I of Sweden was arranged mainly for political reasons.

Soon after conquering the Swedish throne, Gustav wished to marry and cement his claim with an heir. However, due to the disputed origins of his reign and his decision to convert Sweden to the Protestant faith, he had trouble finding suitable matches; he failed repeatedly in his negotiations to marry Dorothea of Denmark, Sophia of Mecklenburg, Anna of Pomerania and Hedwig of Poland.

Though the Duchy of Saxe-Lauenburg was small and poor, it had many advantages: its dynasty was related to some of the most powerful dynasties of Europe, forming useful connections with the German princes; it was Protestant, which was important for the ongoing Swedish Reformation; finally, it had a valuable link to Denmark, as Catherine's older sister, Dorothea, was married to Christian, the Crown Prince of Denmark.

Catherine's wedding to Gustav – seventeen years her senior – was celebrated with great pomp in Stockholm on Catherine's 18th birthday. Historians know very little of Catherine as a person, though legends describe her as cold and melancholic, and her marriage as a stormy and unhappy one. In 1533 she gave birth to the future King Eric XIV, famous for being an unpredictable and melancholic character in his own right.

Catherine's life was cut tragically short in September 1535 when she fell during a ball dance while pregnant with her second child. Her fall confined her to bed and she died shortly after, a day before her twenty-second birthday, her baby unborn. Political opponents of Gustav spread rumours about him beating Catherine to death in a fit of rage, supposedly after hearing reports of her slandering him, but there is no evidence to support this theory. Catherine's skeleton was exhumed in the 1940s and no injuries were found. Her heavy fall was confirmed in a letter by King Christian III of Denmark, an eyewitness and no friend of Gustav.

OLD GALLOWS HILL

A work of art in a grim location

Arabiankatu 1
Arabianranta district, on the northeastern side of the porcelain factory, and on the right-hand side as you turn from Hämeentie to Arabiankatu

In the Arabianranta district, Old Gallows Hill (*Hirsipuukallio* in Finnish), a barely noticeable little cliff, badly chipped away by the roads, resonates with an uneasy atmosphere. For many years it hosted the gallows, which were in active use when Helsinki was a young city centred around the Vanhakaupunki. Old Gallows Hill now plays host to the modern artwork *Lintuparatiisi* (*Bird Paradise*) by Jukka Viberg. It boasts 82 little metal birds, which represent the species nesting in the local Vanhankaupunginlahti bay. Each of them has a tag displaying its scientific Latin name.

The hill at the time was most probably an island, conveniently located out of town. It was known as Galgberget (Gallows-hill in Swedish), as the government and most of the population was Swedish-speaking. It was in use for less than a hundred years, and the population of Helsinki throughout its time was around 500–700 souls, so the gibbet probably saw little use. Most of the people that took the short drop and sudden stop here were thieves and murderers, but sometimes more politically motivated executions took place. In 1599 King Charles IX of Sweden took over the realm and vanquished the former king Sigismund III; ripples of the coup could be felt in the infant city. Charles had nine of Sigismund's loyal underlings hanged here at Old Gallows Hill, including the local bailiff, city scribe and customs official. It is said their troubled souls still haunt the cliff, wailing over their cruel fate.

Finland finally abolished the death penalty in 1950, although in the 20th century it had been only used in wartime. The last person executed during peacetime was the murderer Tahvo Putkonen in 1825; he was decapitated with an axe. After this, death penalties were replaced by banishment to Siberia. The last people to be executed in Finland during wartime were three Soviet spies in 1944, and the last for a civilian crime was the infamous Toivo Koljonen in 1943, for murdering six people.

VALLILA ALLOTMENT GARDEN COTTAGE

The smallest museum in Helsinki

Mansikkapolku 93 in the allotment
Kumpulankatu 1 (official address)
hallitus@vallilanspy.net
June—August, Sunday 1pm—3pm
Free entry

Established in 1932 in a traditional working-class neighbourhood, the Vallila allotment garden is home to one of Finland's smallest museums — in a 10-square metre hut, one of many that was built on the same model in order to ensure a uniform appearance. The cottage was designed by town planning architects Birger Brunila and Väinö Tuukkanen.

The cottage is surrounded by its own garden, planted according to model plans from the 1930s originally designed by the city's garden consultant Elisabeth Koch. Part of it is a traditional flower garden, with areas reserved for fruits and vegetables. Communal meals are prepared from these vegetables for the residents of this active community, who also maintain the museum on a voluntary basis.

Vegetable growing was an important business for the working class in the early decades, sometimes saving families from starvation. Even pigs were farmed in Vallila in the 1940s.

The old gardening tools date from this era, donated by long-time gardeners of Vallila. And the cottage itself is filled with artefacts from the era, including a storm lantern, coffee grinder and a Primus stove.

Allotment gardens

An allotment garden (often simply called an allotment, or a community garden) is a plot of land made available for individual, non-commercial gardening or growing food plants. The oldest allotment site in the world is Great Somerford Free Gardens in the Wiltshire village of Great Somerford (England).

The first allotment garden in Finland was established in 1916 in Tampere, and they began to develop in Helsinki in parallel with urbanisation and industrialisation. Nowadays there are about fifty of them all around Finland.

WORKING CLASS HOME MUSEUM

A time capsule

Kirstinkuja 4
09 3107 1548
June–October, Wednesday–Sunday 11am–5pm
Free entry

Located close to the Linnanmäki amusement park in one of the city's oldest public housing estates (built in 1909), the Working Class Home Museum introduces visitors to the living conditions experienced by Helsinki's labour forces between 1909 and 1985. It's a great place to observe everyday life in Helsinki over the last hundred years.

The little courtyard is a rare example of the wooden architecture of

the working class districts. Built by the city in the early 20th century, the homes were originally meant for large families, which is difficult to imagine when you navigate through the cramped rooms. As wooden buildings lost popularity in the 1950s, the row on Kirstinkuja was earmarked for demolition, to be replaced with modern block houses. But the homes were left to rot and gained a seedy reputation. Salvation came in 1986; the whole complex was restored and preserved as a fine example of old-time Helsinki. The nine small single-room apartments have stoves for cooking, old-fashioned collapsible beds, and are furnished after the fashions of different decades, including a wartime home during the blackout, complete with window shutters to avoid attracting enemy aircraft. The garden is also interesting, with many traditional plant species tended by the museum staff.

STATUE OF KULLERVO

The tragic figure from Kalevala

Kaupunginpuutarha garden
Hammarskjöldintie 1
Visible from behind the fence, but best seen from inside the garden
09 3103 9985
Tuesday 9am–3pm, Wednesday–Friday 12pm–3pm, Saturday–Sunday
12pm–4pm

Inside the beautiful Kaupunginpuutarha garden is a statue of a man with a spade in his hand and a dog at his feet. Created by C.E. Sjöstrand in 1867, the statue represents Kullervo, a famous character in the Finnish national epic *Kalevala*. This is one of the earliest public statues in Helsinki yet not well known: people visiting the garden are usually too distracted by the glorious flora to pay the figure any attention.

A classic tale of tragedy and a life gone horrible wrong, Kullervo's story ends with him making the grimmest of choices. Kullervo is the son of Kalervo, a leader of a tribe. When Kalervo is defeated by a rival family, his infant son, Kullervo, is made a slave, put to herding cattle in the forest. His master's evil wife bakes a stone inside Kullervo's bread, and when Kullervo tries to cut the bread, his knife breaks. The knife was his only keepsake from his father; the breaking of it infuriates Kullervo, who curses and vows revenge.

Kullervo escapes and meets a strange old woman, who tells him that his family is alive. After he finds them, they tell him that his sister is missing.

Later in his journey, Kullervo meets and seduces a girl, only to discover later that the girl is his missing sister. Horrified, the sister throws herself in the rapids and dies.

The self-destructive Kullervo goes to war with his foes, but during a campaign of murder and mayhem he hears that his family has died. Kullervo returns to an empty home, his heart black with despair. He speaks to his blade, mourning how much innocent blood it has spilled, asking if it would now please the sword to drink the blood of the guilty, the blood of Kullervo. Somberly, the blade replies, saying that it gladly takes the life of both the innocent and the guilty. Kullervo drives the sword through himself and dies.

Kullervo and Tolkien

The story of Kullervo had a great impact on J.R.R. Tolkien, who fashioned his story of Túrin Turambar after Kullervo, including the dialogue with the sword.

"Kullervo, son of Kalervo,
Drew his sword, looked at it,
Turned it over, questioning:
Would it please this iron blade
To devour guilty flesh
And to drink the criminal blood?"   (Translation: Eino Friberg)

THE REVOLUTION TABLE

Have a beer with ghosts of the Communist past

Juttutupa bar
Säästöpankinranta 600530
www.juttutupa.com
Monday 10:30am–11pm, Tuesday 10:30am–11pm, Wednesday–Thursday
10:30am–1am, Friday 10:30am–3am, Saturday 11am–3am, Sunday
12pm–11pm
Metro: Hakaniemi

Only frequent customers of the Juttutupa bar in the Paasitorni building know that the round table in the right-hand corner is known as the "Revolution table". One can find Soviet symbols, old pictures of revolutionary figures, and historical information under the protective glass covering the table. Famous communists once schemed here, such as Lenin (although this is disputed) and Otto Ville Kuusinen, who later became the prime minister of the infamous "Terijoki government", a Soviet puppet regime established during the invasion of Karelia in the Winter War.

Built in 1908 as a meeting place for the working class by architect Karl Lindahl, the Paasitorni was the People's House (työväentalo) that sparked the Finnish Civil War.

In January 1918 the relationship between the Red and the White Guards in Finland became extremely strained and war was unavoidable. In late January a red lantern was hoisted to the tower window in Paasitorni to mark the beginning of the war. The building was heavily bombed from the other side of Töölönlahti bay by the German forces during

the conflict. In April 1918, when the Reds had lost the war, a white flag was raised for surrender.

Nowadays, Paasitorni hosts meeting rooms and halls, a hotel and four different restaurants.

Lenin in Helsinki

Lenin stayed in Helsinki, hiding from the authorities, on a number of occasions. On Vuorimiehenkatu 25 a memorial plaque commemorates the time in spring 1906 when he was living here, preparing the Fourth Party Congress of the Russian Social Democratic Labour Party. The plaque was installed in 1970, the period of Finlandisation when relations with the Soviet Union were good.

Another period of Lenin's Finnish exile is remembered in Sörnäisten rantatie 1. He lived here for some time in 1917 when he was hiding from the Russian Provisional Government.

Despite its name, no bank has existed in Säästöpankinranta. The area gets its name from a restaurant that used to exist here, and the fact that Helsinkiites used to carry so much money to the restaurant it ended up being called *Säästöpankki* (Savings Bank).

HARJU YOUTH HOUSE

A house built in a former mortuary

Aleksis Kiven katu 1-3
Metro: Sörnäinen

If you look carefully at Harju Youth House you'll notice a few details that are not common to such places: above the main entrance and two white Christian crosses on the brick walls, a Latin phrase reads "Statutum est hominibus mori" (a variation of Paul: Letters to the Hebrews 9:27, "It is established that men only die once").

Designed by architect Albert Nyberg, the house was in fact first built as a mortuary in 1922. Bodies were washed here, put into coffins and loaded onto a funerary train that went to Malmi cemetery: it left from the back yard, where you can still see the dignified doorway for the departure.

The trains usually left twice weekly and were decorated with white crosses and spruce branches. They originally had two coaches for bodies and four for mourning relatives, priests and other people visiting the graveyard. Later, the living and the dead travelled separately. Passengers were issued special tickets marked with a cross, and the trains drove to the cemetery under less steam than usual, so that the noise wouldn't disrupt the funerals.

The mortuary closed down in the mid-1950s when the trains were made redundant by motorisation. It functioned as a paint warehouse for decades but was finally abandoned completely. Drifters and other homeless people settled in the building to escape the winter cold, and the building was left to decay until the mid-1980s when it was occupied by a group of youngsters from the neighbourhood. The former mortuary was renovated, refurbished and opened as a youth house in 1986.

SOMPASAUNA

A fantastic free sauna open 24 hours a day

Sompasaaren laituri
sompasauna@sompasauna.fi.
Open 24/7
Free entry

Sompasauna is a free, public sauna in a shanty cottage in an isolated harbour area of Sompasaari, south of the Kalasatama district. It is also close to the Korkeasaari Zoo, and the sound of roaring lions can sometimes be heard over the sea.

Sompasauna was set up in 2011 when a group of men found a small wood-burning sauna stove and decided to put it to use. They built a shack sauna (without permits) in the depths of an old harbour. The sauna was free to all, and in the first year, Sompasauna attracted hundreds of people. Its reputation spread quickly. The sauna was an underground hit, though its original creators soon moved on.

Some of the people who attended Sompasauna in the first summer went on to upgrade it further. In the summer of 2012 they redesigned and rebuilt the sauna while still upholding the original vision of its creators. They used only discarded materials and stuff they had found while dumpster diving. Other interested parties also contributed donations.

In 2013 the city of Helsinki tore down the sauna due to its lack of a permit. But in the fall of the same year, the people behind the new Sompasauna project registered an official association to promote the culture of public saunas and Sompasauna was built again.

From its early beginnings, Sompasauna has promoted the ideals of free, mixed-sex public sauna for everyone. The only restrictions are that children can't use the sauna without adults, and you can't go to the sauna when severely drunk. The sauna is open 24 hours a day, free of charge and cannot be reserved.

A SACRIFICIAL STONE

Art and architecture gems inside the zoo

Korkeasaari Zoo
Mustikkamaanpolku 12
www.korkeasaari.fi
Daily, October—March 10am—4pm, April 10am—6pm; May—August 10am—8pm, September 10am—6pm

Over half a million people visit the Korkeasaari Zoo annually, but few know about the historical sights within. The zoo, located on its own 24-hectare island, was founded in 1889 by a local distillery company. After Prohibition laws were set, the company went bankrupt and in 1920 the zoo passed to the city of Helsinki.

A number of notable architects designed buildings for the island in the early 1900s. The tiny Karhulinna (Bear castle) cage is by Theodor Höijer and dates from 1903. There is a slightly larger former polar bear cage near the ferry terminal, which dates from 1914 and was home to these arctic beasts until 1955. The current concrete Karhulinna houses brown bears and dates from the Olympic year 1952. There are no longer any polar bears in the zoo, and both of the old bear castles of Korkeasaari now host art galleries.

The only known prehistoric sacrificial stone (*kuppikivi*) in Helsinki was found in Korkeasaari in 2013 by an amateur archaeologist. About two metres long and a metre in height, it is in a rocky area on the highest point of the island, near the enclosures of the snow leopards and the Finnish forest reindeers. There is a good view towards Suomenlinna from this location. Expert estimates date it to the Bronze Age, possibly about 3500 years ago.

There are about 350 known kuppikivi stones in Finland, most of which date from the late Iron Age and are located near agricultural land. Some of them were still in use until the 20th century. They are basically boulders that have small round cups carved into them, hence their name (*kuppi* = cup). Offerings such as grain and milk were left in the cups for forefathers, elves and goblins to ensure future fortunes in quarry and crops alike. Some also believed that the rainwater in the cups had magical potency.

> The zoo was originally intended to be built in Alppila, hence the name of the district, Eläintarha, meaning "zoo".

NEARBY

A statue that was exhibited at the Paris World Fair of 1889 ⑲

The bronze statue *Pukki* (*The Billy Goat*), stands in front of the eponymous restaurant at the centre of the Korkeasaari island. The figure has remained relatively unfamiliar to local residents, as the zoo offers so many other distractions. The lifelike statue hails from Italy and was designed by the Milanese artist Constantino Pandiani. It was originally brought to Finland from the Paris World Fair of 1889. Pandiani's other public statues are scattered around Italy, so *The Billy Goat* of Korkeasaari remains a rare example of his work in the far north.

KIVINOKKA'S GARDEN

A small Eden within the capital

Kulosaari and Herttoniemi Metro station
From Kulosaari Metro station, take Kulosaaren puistotie to the east.
From Herttoniemi Metro station, take Hiihtäjäntie and enter the trails leading to the area at Hiihtäjäntie 4
The cabins closest to the road are visible from the Metro but the scenic sites are farther afield

Part of the nature oasis of Vanhankaupunginlahti bay, the Kivinokka area is a pleasant marine environment in which to spend a summer day. There is a nature trail with a birdwatching tower (wheelchair accessible and with information in braille) and a bird hide nearby.

The allotment garden of Kivinokka itself is a beautiful place of serene nature in the middle of Helsinki. It is an interesting contrast of tranquil scenery and gruesome tales.

The garden has its beginnings in 1907, when the garden city of Kulosaari was founded. The workers associations wanted to offer a healthier life during the summer for the labourers living in their chronically cramped quarters. The workers' summer huts were usually dismantled for the winter, but due to the lack of men during the Second World War, they were left in place and afterwards were allowed to remain there permanently. Some of them were also inhabited year-round after the war because of a shortage in housing. There are now over 800 cabins, some on the community garden and some scattered throughout the forests.

One notable feature of Kivinokka was its old-fashioned *tanssilava* (dance hall), where the well-known dance orchestra Dallapé was founded in 1925. Famous Finnish musicians such as Georg Malmstén, Kauko Käyhkö and Vili Vesterinen performed in Dallapé. A memorial stone for the orchestra is in the western part of the peninsula.

Though the area is beautiful, in the 1990s it was the scene of the story of a local arsonist called Ismo Junni who set fire to several of the huts out of spite — he was jealous of their owners and wanted one for himself. His signature traits included burning his victims to death in their own huts, as well as occasionally taking some of their teeth for his collection, earning him the moniker "teethmurderer of Katajanokka". Junni was convicted of killing a total of five persons.

Confusingly, the historical Kulosaari Manor, founded in the 1500s, is not located in Kulosaari island but in Kivinokka on the other side of the narrow strait. Its most famous owner was Augustin Ehrensvärd, the designer of Suomenlinna. A Freemason, Ehrensvärd often gathered his fellow brethren to admire the sea fortress from the highest point of Kulosaari. The main building was designed by C.L. Engel and dates from the 1810s.

WORKMEN OF HERTTONIEMI FIGURES

Contemporary art in an industrial area

The street signs are on a large area between Itäväylä, Linnanrakentajantie and Sahaajankatu
Metro: Herttoniemi

After the summer of 2014, many residents were puzzled to see little figures sprouting up around Herttoniemi industrial area, decorating the street signage. Was this a new wave of contemporary guerrilla art?

Designed by two artists, Sirpa Hynninen and Vesa-Ville Saarinen, these figures are in fact public artwork commissioned by the Helsinki Art Museum. They are called *Herttoniemen duunarit* (*Workmen of Hert-toniemi*). The artwork is scattered around almost sixty places, on the street signage between Itäväylä, Sahaajankatu and Linnanrakentajantie, in this old industrial zone.

Made of weatherproof steel and painted black, the figures depict workmen with their tools. Each tiny steel man reflects a street name, all of which are related to industries and enterprises: Sahaajankatu (Sawyer Street) has a man with a saw; Lämmittäjänkuja (Boilerman Alley) has a man with a spade; and even Teollisuusneuvoksenkatu (Industry Advisor Street) has a large man in a top hat. Many of the occupations represented are dying out or have already become redundant.

JAPANESE GARDEN
OF ROIHUVUORI

A peaceful place

Roihuvuorentie 12–16
The cherry blossom park is at the nearby hillside leading to the mushroom-shaped water tower, east of Sahaajankatu
Metro: Herttoniemi

Designed according to the principles of oriental garden architecture, the Japanese Garden of Roihuvuori occupies nine hectares, divided into four subsections named after the four symbols of the Chinese constellations: the gardens of the Vermillion Bird, the Azure Dragon, the White Tiger and the Black Turtle (Japanese garden architecture was largely influenced by Chinese garden culture). The Azure dragon marks the east, spring and morning; the Vermillion Bird is the symbol of south, summer and midday; the White Tiger represents west, autumn and evening; and the Black Turtle is the symbol of north, winter and midnight.

The garden has traditional bamboo fences and canopies, a moon gate, rock and sand arrangements, and a stream. A slate quarry was in operation here until the 1950s, which explains the sharp cliff edges.

The garden was constructed during the Finnish economic recession of the early 1990s as a public project to engage unemployed builders. It had initially been planned as a dedication to the Soviet leader Mikhail Gorbachev (like the Lenin Park in Alppila) and fashioned in an austere style, but as the Soviet Union fell during the construction, the park began to look more Japanese and was finally completed in this style. All things Japanese were quite fashionable in 1990s Finland due to the arrival of karaoke and the incredibly popular *Moomin* animated TV series.

Japanese gardens were originally sacred places around the residences and temples of the privileged. They are usually fenced with stone walls and include five traditional elements (also present in *Roihuvuori*): a pond, waterfall, stream

islands, rocks, and real or symbolic trees.

Spring is a great time to visit the garden, which has numerous cherry blossoms (*hanami* in Japanese). A hanami celebration is held annually in the nearby cherry park. The 250 cherries growing here are Sargent's cherries (Prunus sargentii). The celebrations have origami presentations, traditional dance and music, ikebana flower art, budo, tea ceremonies and Japanese cuisine on sale. The celebration is the perfect time to picnic in the park.

MEMORIAL STONE FOR A RIDING HORSE ㉓

The oldest public memorial in the city

Puotilantie 7
The memorial is west of the manor house and the chapel, in the forested park on the hill, south of Puotilantie
Metro: Puotila

On the grounds of Puotila Manor, the intriguing pile of stones lying west of the house and the chapel is the so-called "memorial stone for a riding horse".

It is said to be the oldest public memorial in the city.

Legend says that the former lord of the manor, Johan Erik Lindroos, buried his favourite riding horse and a dog at this precise spot in June 1862, indicated by an inscription on the stone pedestal.

There also used to be a stone chalice on the memorial, which was unfortunately stolen in the 1960s.

Dating from the 1600s, Puotila (Botby) Manor was governed for centuries by the famous noble families of Jägerhorn and Cronstedt. The troops of Peter the Great burned the old building down in the early 1700s, and the current one was built around 1800. It now houses a restaurant.

The neo-Gothic former granary (1859) near the main building was converted to a very popular wedding chapel in 1963.

The manor house is said to be haunted by a restless white lady, the spirit of Birgitta Jägerhorn. She is supposedly waiting in vain for her fiancé, who fell in the infamous Battle of Poltava during the Great Northern War of 1709. Birgitta likes to wander around the parkland and along the secret tunnel connecting the granary and the main building.

MEDIEVAL HILLFORT

The oldest man-made building in Helsinki

Linnavuorentie 5
From Varjakanvalkama road, turn left to Linnavuorentie. Between the houses
you'll see a trail leading to the informational plaque and up the hill to the fort

Around 30 metres above the sea, in the middle of a residential area close to Vartionkylänlahti, stands a hillfort from the Iron Age. It is the only one in Helsinki and a good example of its kind.

A hillfort is a fortification built on a high hill or a cliff. They usually have primitive walls and rudimentary barricades built from stone and wood, often constructed by simply piling up the materials. The remains of the wall of Helsinki's hillfort is about two to four metres wide and around 25–50 centimetres tall.

Hillforts were common in the Bronze and Iron Ages before people began building proper castles and fortresses. In Europe there are few thousand hillforts, of which about a hundred are located in Finland. Some hillforts represent the oldest remaining structures created by Europeans. Helsinki's hillfort is no exception; if you don't count the few burial mounds, the hillfort is the oldest man-made building in Helsinki.

Although the precise age of Helsinki's hillfort is not known, it's at least from the early Middle Ages, probably even older than that. The oldest findings from the area are arrowheads dated to the Stone Age, around 3000 BC, when the area was covered by water and the hillfort was an island.

According to a folk tale, the hillfort was built by the Viking king Helsing while his brothers Sibbe and Borg built the hillforts of Sibbesborg (now in Sipoo) and Porvoo (Borgå in Swedish).

Although the story of the Viking king has no historical evidence to support it, the hillfort was nonetheless important in ancient times. When Vuosaari was still an island, the fort offered an ideal point from which to observe the seas and defend against any enemies.

About four kilometres west from Vuosaari is Vartiosaari (The Guardian Island), which acted as a lookout point for the hillfort (see page 212).

A man-made hill for bird watchers

Access via multiple pathways starting from Satamakaari and Niinisaarentie

Vuosaaren täyttömäki is a strange hill in the otherwise flat landscape of Eastern Helsinki: over 65-metres-high, it was made with over six million cubic metres of soil from the nearby Vuosaari Harbour construction site and the former Vuosaari dumping ground (in operation between 1966–1988, it was the second biggest dump in Scandinavia after the Ämmässuo dumping ground in Espoo).

This artificial hill is still under development and the network of trails will be refined in the future. However, it already offers great views of the whole city, and of Vuosaari Harbour in particular. It is also popular with local birdwatchers who come here to witness the Arktika (the annual bird migration to the Arctic regions). Vegetation on the hill was collected from all over the coasts and transferred here, as were the numerous stones, which originate from Helsinki construction yards.

Other peculiarities are the ravine near the top (which looks man-made), some "planted" dead pine trees (kelohonka), a wild-strawberry (Fragaria vesca) field and a small marshy pond.

Among the exhibits of the hill is the stump of the willow of Lasipalatsi (see page 104), a legendary tree in downtown Helsinki that fell down in 2003. The stump should be visible on the hill for as long as the timber withstands the weather.

Near the edge of the forest on the eastern slope is part of the Krepost Sveaborg (see page 132).

To the South-East

THE CHAPEL OF KULOSAARI CEMETERY

A little-known cemetery with a distinctive chapel

Leposaarentie
09 2340 2980
Daily 7am—10pm
Metro: Kulosaari

Kulosaari cemetery is located on a small island called Leposaari (The Isle of Rest). Not many people know it's there, but if you pay attention, you may glimpse the cemetery while travelling through Kulosaari by metro.

Although Kulosaari Cemetery is the smallest in the Helsinki region (only 1,500 graves), it has its share of famous names, such as the athlete and five-time Olympic medalist Hannes Kolehmainen, as well as the former Assistant Secretary-General of the United Nations, Kurt Jansson.

One of the most distinct features of the graveyard is the strange, octagonal chapel designed by the architect Armas Lindgren, who also played a major role in the general design of the cemetery. When Lindgren passed away in 1929 he was buried here and architect Arne Helander continued his work, designing features such as the iron gates. The chapel is open only during services.

The history of Kulosaari Cemetery dates back to the days when Kulosaari was an independent municipality. In 1907 a group of architects came together and formed the joint stock company AB Brändö Villastad. The company's aim was to create a modern villa community in the then unpopulated isle of Kulosaari. The idea was realised in 1922 when Kulosaari gained its independence from the larger municipality of rural Helsinki. Kulosaari remained independent for over 20 years, until it was assimilated to be a part of the city of Helsinki in 1946.

The planning of the cemetery began in 1921, a year before Kulosaari claimed its status as an independent municipality. The then unpopulated isle of Iso-Pässi (The Big Ram) was chosen for the location of the new cemetery and renamed Leposaari. One of the reasons for choosing Iso-Pässi was that the isle had large, magnificent spruces, which the architects thought would compliment the planned chapel. Sadly, during the building process, the builders managed to damage the trees' roots and kill off most of the grove.

The cemetery was inaugurated in 1928. A day after the inauguration ceremony, local housewife Anna Kuosmanen died and became the first person to be buried in the new cemetery. The cemetery remains in use to this day, reserved for Kulosaari inhabitants.

HERTTONIEMENRANTA'S IRON AGE BURIAL MOUND

A hidden ancient tomb

Sorsaniemenpuisto Park
Herttoniemenranta neighborhood
Trails start from nearby streets Sorsavuorenraitti and Sorsavuorenkatu
Metro: Herttoniemi

In suburban Sorsaniemenpuisto park, at the highest point of the hill, a pile of rocks lies at the base of a tree. If you investigate, it becomes evident that the mound is not natural, but artificial. A nearby plaque indicates that the stones are in fact an ancient tomb, hidden in plain sight and unknown to many.

In ancient times, Finns used to bury their warlords on coastal mounds composed of loads and loads of cobblestones. Although some of the most notable examples of these cairns are a bit farther afield (like the impressive UNESCO World Heritage site Sammallahdenmäki in Satakunta), several of them are only a small metro trip away from the centre of Helsinki. The most secret of them lies here, hidden within a residential area of Herttoniemenranta.

The mound dates from the early Iron Age around 1000 BCE. It was excavated in 1886 by the archaeologist J.R. Aspelin, who found burned bones and the tooth of a horse. Many of the neighbouring barrows were destroyed during this period for building material, but fortunately the one in Sorsaniemi survived.

NEARBY
Two further burial mounds ③

There are two more mounds visible from the metro if you know where to look. One Herttoniemi grave is at the meeting point of Hitsaajankatu and Suolakivenkatu. Another grave lies in Kulosaari, just west of the Kulosaari metro station, beside the rails.

Tombs in stone cairns

Though practiced in Scandinavia as late as the Iron Age, burying the dead in a stone cairn dates back to the Stone Age. The burial mound custom is unknown in inner Finland, which suggests that it is borrowed from the coastally influential Scandinavian culture. In inner parts of Finland, the dead were burned then buried in the ground. Though some mounds have been found to contain intact remains, most of these rocky graves were used to house only the ashes of the deceased, especially in the later ages. Most of the graves were located by the sea; some had weapons, goods and jewellery buried within, which is the reason why they were often plundered by grave robbers. Burial mounds had an important place in Nordic paganism. The Vikings believed that by burning the dead, the soul could be transferred to Valhalla. The mounds were also places of ancestor worship among the ancient Nordic cultures. Because the building of a cairn was a demanding task, it was reserved for the powerful members of the society. The mounds were often erected in high places on the coast.

THE CURSED MANSION OF HERTTONIEMI

Ghosts and traitors

Linnanrakentajantie 12
09 789874
May–September, Sunday 12pm–2pm
Guided tours at 2pm
October–April, open every first Sunday

Built in the 16th century (though it gained its current look in the 19th century under vice-admiral Carl Olof Cronstedt), the Herttoniemi Mansion has been supposedly haunted since Cronstedt's actions in the

Finnish War (1808–1809). As the commander of Viapori, he surrendered the fortress without firing a shot at the besieging Russians.

According to the story, the Russians were outnumbered, but they managed to convince Cronstedt to surrender for a large amount of gold. Swedish courts sentenced Cronstedt to death in absentia for high treason, but he was later pardoned and rewarded by the czar. According to one tale, Cronstedt was supposed to get two barrels full of gold, but the Russians tricked him; under the top layer of gold coins there was nothing but sand. Shamed by his treachery and gullibility, Cronstedt sank the barrels in a strait between Herttoniemi and Laajasalo. That is the reason why, according to legend, the cursed strait will never freeze.

Others whisper that Cronstedt actually got his gold and that he hid it in the foundations of the mansion. Whatever the case, people have reported seeing the ghost of Cronstedt walking the grounds, weeping over his accursed fate. Historians have found no hard evidence to support the story of Cronstedt's betrayal. There have been many theories surrounding the surrender: the equipment in Viapori was poor; the men didn't respond well to Cronstedt; and the gunpowder reserves were near empty. Though Cronstedt may have been innocent, there is another tale that might explain the ghastly legends.

The last private owner of the mansion, Johan Bergbom, was murdered in the Finnish Civil War when Russian-supported Red forces looted the mansion in search of weapons and precious goods. Bergbom was killed at the breakfast table. His widow, Helene Gustava Bergbom, later donated the mansion to an association in order to establish a museum for Finnish-Swedish culture, similar to Seurasaari. The project never materialised, but the windmill and farmhouses date from this period. Interestingly, the two garden villas were probably designed by C.L. Engel, the architect of Helsinki Cathedral and the Empire-style city centre.

THE LITTLE-KNOWN WONDERS OF VARTIOSAARI

A stone labyrinth, a mysterious church and a Viking lookout point

In winter you can walk across the ice. In summer take the ferry operated
by Suomen saaristokuljetus from Laajasalo (the end of Reposaarentie) or
Hakaniemi
Follow the nature trail to find the sights

Vartiosaari (The Guardian Island) is a picturesque island that has remained almost untouched. Though Vartiosaari is inhabited by roughly twenty residents, it is not well known; most people living in Helsinki are familiar with it as a name on the map but have never visited. This is a pity, since the island is home to several interesting features: a stone labyrinth, a mysterious outdoor church, and an old Viking lookout point.

Arriving on the island, a signposted trail leads around Vartiosaari. Following it, you will first find an outdoor area with a large wooden cross. There is also wood and stone serving as church pews. Located in an old slate mine, Metsäkirkko (Forest Church) became an outdoor church in 2002. Slate from the mine was originally used for the construction of Suomenlinna sea fortress.

Soon after the church, as you continue towards the Viking lookout point, you will find a stone labyrinth known as a *jatulintarha* (giant's garden). Most of these labyrinths are ancient (they appear to date from medieval times), but the one in Vartiosaari is a modern one, built using stone from the slate mine. Historians are unsure of the motives for building a *jatulintarha*.

After the labyrinth, you'll reach a crossroads with a distinctive spruce. This is tapionpöytä (Tapio's table – scientific name *Picae abiens f. tabulaeformis*), a dwarf form of the common spruce, and a reminder of the ancient times when pagan Finns used to leave offerings for the forest god Tapio on these kinds of trees.

As you move towards the other end of the island, you will reach a cliff where you can easily observe the whole sea. In olden times this was used as a lookout point by the Vikings, some of whom lived in the coastal areas. Ships could be seen coming from miles away. The sea area around Vartiosaari has always been an important route for ships travelling in the Gulf of Finland, which made Vartiosaari a good place for preparing both defence and raids. The stone pyramid here is not as ancient but is a *kummeli* (sea cairn) from the Russian period.

YLISKYLÄ'S PINE TREE

A sacred tree near a shopping mall

Muurahaisenpolku Street
Next to the Saari shopping centre
Metro: Herttoniemi
Buses: 84, 85, 86 and 88 towards Laajasalo

Shopping malls are hardly the places to find ancient relics. Yet the commercial centre of Yliskylä offers a surprise: the majestic umbrella-shaped pine tree is an authentic example of Finnish tree worship, rooted in paganism.

Known as "haltiamänty", the elf pine used to belong to nearby Uppby manor house (its Swedish name, although nowadays it is mostly known by its Finnish name, Yliskylä). The distinctive old tree was held as the sacred protector of the manor family.

In the glory days of the house, the pine was honoured with offerings of various foodstuffs on important annual occasions, such as harvest, when the first grains were sacrificed to it. These traditions ended when the fields and meadows of Uppby were sold off to make way for the growing capital's needs. Dense urban cityscape has long since replaced the agrarian landscape in which the pine tree sprouted.

The manor of Uppby owned vast lands in Laajasalo. Many agricultural buildings were pulled down during the construction of the mall in the 1960s and only a small cottage survived: the yellow Ylistalo communal centre near the pine. Fortunately, the sacred tree was saved and has been a symbol for Yliskylä ever since.

Ancient tree worship was practised in Finland for millennia. Trees were believed to be linked to a supernatural landlord, known by various terms such as *haltia* (elf) and *tonttu* (gnome). The Finnish *tonttu* and the Swedish *tomte* are related to the words *tontti* (Finnish) and *tomt* (Swedish), both meaning "building sites".

If the elf was treated with respect, the house had good fortune in crops, cattle and employees. It was taboo to harm a sacred tree; cutting a branch was forbidden and felling was considered mortally dangerous for the associated household. Some folk also believed their sacred tree worked as a kind of astral portal, through which they could contact their ancestors.

Sometimes the trees were used in traditional healing rites, when a sick person was directed to touch the bark, or newborn babies were blessed at the tree. A mother might make an offering of her first drops of milk.

Despite the nation's supposed Christianity, tree worship was common until the 1800s; the two were intangibly intermingled, with sacrifices made during Christian holy days. But with urbanisation in the 1900s, tree worship fell gradually from favour, though it can still be found in modern form when commemorative trees are planted for births, betrothals and marriages.

THE KAGAAL STONE

A reminder of a secret meeting held to fight Russification

Killingholmanpolku
Tullisaari park
Metro: Herttoniemi then bus 88 towards Laajasalo

Kagaalin kivi (*the Kagaal stone*) is an obelisk erected during the Russification era, when the Finns showed resistance to the Russian imperial approaches. The text in the granite says in Swedish and Finnish: "On 3rd August in the year 1903", and nothing more, due to fear of persecution at the time. The date refers to the meeting held in Tullisaari Manor attended by notable Finns, including future president P.E. Svinhufvud. Originally scheduled to happen at Hotel Kämp, it was transferred to Laajasalo, considered far enough from the capital to be safe (an hour by steamer at the time).

During the Russification era the politically active Finns were divided between the supporters of conciliatory policy and opponents of the Russification, or constitutionalists.

The name "Kagaal" comes from a Hebrew word meaning a congregation, kahal. Russian nationalists used it as a pejorative term for Jewish secret societies, and later for the constitutional associations of the Grand Duchy. The Kagaal in question organised draft strikes. These eventually led to the Czar abandoning the draft of Finnish citizens.

The Russification of Finland (1899–1905 and 1908–1917), called "sortokaudet"/"sortovuodet" ("times"/"years of oppression"), was a governmental policy of the Russian Empire aimed at terminating the Grand Duchy's political autonomy. It was part of a larger policy pursued by late 19th to early 20th century Russian governments that tried to abolish the autonomy of non-Russian minorities. The Russification campaigns provoked Finnish resistance, starting with petitions, escalating to strikes and eventually active resistance. The opposition to Russification was one of the main factors that ultimately led to Finland's declaration of independence in 1917.

NEARBY
Aino Acktén huvila

(8)

The striped wooden villa from 1877 that stands next to the stone is called "Aino Acktén huvila" (villa). Ackté (1876–1944) was the country's first international star and opera pioneer, Salome being her favourite role. She worked in Paris and New York. The villa appeared in the 1983 Hollywood thriller *Gorky Park*, when Helsinki once again acted as a surrogate for Moscow due to its Russian-era architecture (and the Soviet Union being out of limits to Western cinematographers).

ENGRAVING FOR A DROWNED FISHERMAN

A discreet reminder

Kruunuvuori
Bus: 88 from Herttoniemi metro station
From the final stop of bus 88, continue along Päätie and walk uphill.
The engraving is at the bottom of the sea cliffs on the southwestern corner.
It is difficult to spot, but can be found near some more modern inscriptions,
just a little higher on the grey stone

Kruunuvuori is at the end of the road in Laajasalo. After passing through the well-to-do residential area of Kaitalahti, the road turns into a muddy track that climbs uphill through a forest to a real nature paradise with sea views to the city.

One lonely seaside cliff bears a beautiful inscription in Swedish that predates the villa community. Dedicated to a lost soul, it reads: "F. Friberg, drunknad 18.8.1869". The inscription, done by an unknown friend, informs visitors that a fisherman named F. Friberg drowned here on 18 August 1869.

Kruunuvuori was originally separated from Uppby Manor's grounds and sold to German consul Albert Goldbeck-Löwe in 1913. There had been a villa community since the late 1800s, which was expanded after the purchase. During this golden age, the villas were serviced by a steamboat link to Pohjoisranta in the city centre, just a short hop across the sea.

The original residents were mostly of German descent, but in 1944 the ownership abruptly passed to the Soviet Union and through it to the Communist Party of Finland. Communist activists and their families spent their summers in the old villas built by their German predecessors. In 1955 the area was purchased by the industrialist Aarne Aarnio, who spent the following decades trying to get construction permits for blockhouses. The City of Helsinki refused these, and the villas continued to be used by employees of Aarnio's company. The residents vanished one by one between the 1980s and 2000s, and all that remains now are old flower beds, garden plants, ruins and a few dilapidated buildings.

The nature of Kruunuvuori is exemplified by bare cliffs bordering the sea and lush green forests. The highlight of the visit is the beautiful Kruunuvuorenlampi pond in the middle. This is a paradise for both waterfowl and flora that requires wilderness conditions.

NEARBY

A dog's grave in Tullisaari ⑩

Metro: Herttoniemi – Bus: 88 – Tullisaari 2

Tullisaari Manor Park hosted many wooden villas during its heyday in the 1800s and early 1900s. The first villa was built for local politician Leonard Borgström (1832–1907) and his family in 1870. The villa had a prominent location on top of the hill near the sea, close to the manor house itself. It was demolished in the 1970s when the park was in a run-down state, but the ruins near the Kagaali stone and Aino Ackté villa, a few hundred metres to the west, on top of the hill facing the sea, were dug up during later park restorations. Near the ruins is a small gravestone with the engraving in English: "Faithful little Tim - 1908". Tim was the pet dog of Borgstrom and his English wife Alice Travers. The Tullisaari manor house itself burned down in 1958; the ruins can be seen in the park.

OIL SILO 468

A stunning light installation

Koirasaarentie
*Open certain weekends in September and October: check www.facebook.com/
Kruunuvuorenranta/ or websites such as www.myhelsinki.com for dates*
Free entry
Bus: 84, 88 from Herttoniemi metro station

In the middle of the growing Kruunuvuorenranta suburb, a strange round building surprises visitors, curious about the numerous holes punched through its grey walls. Formerly an oil silo, "Oil silo 468" is a stunning art installation from local artist group Lightning Design Collective. Led by light artist Tapio Rosenius, the group has transformed the building into an urban light installation incorporating a total of 2,012 holes. The piece was created as part of the World Design Capital Helsinki 2012 project, hence the number of holes.

When the sun is high and daylight shines through the circular holes, a fantastic flicker of shadows is created on the interior walls. After sunset, lights are activated and turn on and off in reaction to the wind. The lights are white during the early evening and turn progressively red at night.

Kruunuvuori was a working oil harbour for almost a century. In 1914 German businessman Albert Goldbeck-Löwe bought the area in order to establish a base for his Finnish shipping business (Kissinge, later Algol). Goldbeck-Löwe also owned a prominent part of the nearby eponymous villa community, of which some vestiges remain.

In 1990 the city council of Helsinki decided to demolish the old oil harbour and create a municipal district. Most of the old industrial buildings have been torn down, but the silo still remains within the growing cityscape.

SUUDELMA WOOD SCULPTURE

Art blended with nature

Fontainebleau Forest
Stansvikintie
Bus: 84 — Gunillantie

As you approach the remote Stansvik Manor you'll pass through a handsome alley of huge oaks. In the stump of a tree in the middle of the alley you'll find a surprising relief of a dreamy-looking couple. Called *Suudelma* (*Kiss*) by the artist Sanna Karlsson-Sutisna, this artwork was sculpted in situ with her instrument of choice: a chainsaw. Don't wait too long to admire this piece of poetry in the forest: nobody knows how long the relief will withstand the climate.

The relief is sculpted on the stump of a maple tree, but the alley is mostly made of oaks planted in the 1860s, grown from acorns imported from Fontainebleau Forest, near Paris, a former hunting park for French kings.

Don't forget to visit the very end of the trail, starting at the edge of the forest on the yard. The manor sits on a narrow esker peninsula (*harjuniemi*), shaped during the Ice Age, like so many natural formations in the country. Most eskers (long sand and gravel ridges) formed within ice-walled tunnels by streams that flowed within and underneath glaciers. The peninsula ends dramatically with beautiful sea views to the Santahamina military zone.

The Teerisaari island (in Santahamina, see page 226) on the opposite side is actually a continuation of the same ridge, which drops underwater here.

Built in 1804, the manor house of Stansvik is one of the oldest in Helsinki. It had previously been a tenant farm for Degerö Manor. The designers avoided the "window tax" legislation that was effective between 1743 and 1810 by using fake windows on the backside of the manor so they could place more on the front to give the impression of wealth. The manor house played host to the completion of one of the most important historical paintings in Finland, *Porvoon valtiopäivät* (*Diet of Porvoo*) by Emanuel Thelning in 1812. There is an impressive Empire-style pier and boathouse next to the manor. Nowadays, the building is a summer residence for employees of the City of Helsinki.

JOLLAS SWAMP

A well-hidden gem of natural beauty

About Hevossalmentie 30
Metro: Herttoniemi then bus 85 or 86 towards Jollas

Jollaksen räme (Jollas swamp) is a little 3.5 hectare wildlife oasis that sits in a suburban area between Furuvikintie and Purjetuulentie. It is about six kilometres from the city centre as the crow flies, but close to twenty when you approach by land.

An informational plaque at the entrance reveals the natural wonders of the place, such as cloudberries, the delicious arctic berry. Unfortunately, you mostly see just cloudberry flowers, as the actual berries are not often produced here. Local wildlife includes hares and foxes, although they can be quite shy animals.

This wet environment can be easily explored via a series of duckboard pathways that form a loop of roughly half a kilometre.

Next to the Jollas swamp is the old villa and the public beach of Furuvik, with stellar views of the sea. This is a good place for a stroll, especially in the summer, and a truly wonderful haven of nature in the middle of a city.

NEARBY
Matosaari island ⑭

Enchanting Matosaari (Worm island) is at the end of the road in southern Jollas. After passing through some of the most expensive estates in the city, you'll find this small island that is linked to its larger neighbour by a causeway. Offering breathtaking sea views, serene Matosaari is home to several historical sights.

On the eastern shore lie the remains of a Russian coastal battery dating from the Crimean War (1855–1856), when the strait of Hevossalmi had to be defended against a possible English invasion. The fortifications were part of a larger defence plan spreading to both sides of the strait, including Teerisaari (in Santahamina, see page 226). The artillery battery was in operation until 1884, when it passed into civilian use.

Landscape gardener Paul Olsson (1890–1973) designed both the villa and the park that can be seen today. He reused the natural stone walls of the fortress in parts of his garden plan. Olsson's villa was destroyed by fire in 1963 and was never rebuilt.

The wooden villa on the northern side of the island dates from the end of the 19th century.

THE TREASURES OF SANTAHAMINA

Centuries of military history

www.santahamina.fi
Visits are by appointment-only tours and on special occasions
Valid passports are required from both foreigners (with a background check)
and Finnish citizens
Metro: Herttoniemi then bus 86

If you are able to visit Santahamina military zone (see opposite page for access information), you'll be highly rewarded with numerous historical wonders from the last two centuries. Unsurprisingly, many war-related memorials are scattered throughout the island. One is the cemetery of the Red prisoners of war. In 1918 over a thousand prisoners died in the camps of Suomenlinna, Santahamina and Isosaari of disease, famine and execution. The mass grave was left unattended until 1949 when the post-war political atmosphere allowed the cemetery to be cleaned up and a memorial built. The sombre relief depicts a fallen soldier, his grieving wife and his son, picking up the revolutionary flag.

Located next to the main road is an older memorial to the Russian officers who died in the Sveaborg rebellion in 1906. It is said that the top of the memorial used to bear the double-headed Romanov eagle, but this was lost a long time ago. Nearby, within the red brick barracks, is a replica of the memorial to Joutselkä. Joutselkä (in Kivennapa, Karelian isthmus) was the battleground of Swedish (and Finnish) forces and Russians in 1555, during the Russo-Swedish War (1554–1557). A memorial pyramid was built by Finns in 1931, but destroyed by Soviets in 1963. This replica was built in 1981 in Santahamina.

In the National Defence University campus is another memorial pyramid, similar to but much older than the Joutselkä pyramid. This is dedicated to the 63 Russian soldiers who died in the Crimean War. It is sited on top of an earlier cemetery, with burials from at least the 18th century, when the island was just a small village. The surrounding buildings of the National Defence University (Kadettikoulu) are impressive examples of Bauhaus-style functionalism, originally built for the accommodation of Finnish athletes in the cancelled 1940 Helsinki Olympic Games. Note the reliefs featuring the lion of Finland's coat of arms, and the 1930s-style helmets on the exterior, similar to those worn by the Wehrmacht.

Apart from the official memorials, Santahamina also offers mementos of past military activity that are harder to notice. Numerous 19th-century inscriptions by Russian soldiers litter the cliffs near the gate to the island and in Leipurinniemi. They are similar to the more accessible scribbles in Sisä-Hattu, Lauttasaari. There are also many notable Crimean War and Krepost Sveaborg battlements in various parts of the island.

The sandy training area in the middle of the island (called Sahara) originated as a Russian firing range in the 1800s. In the first years of Finnish independence it served as an airfield for the rudimentary planes of the era.

VALLISAARI'S RUSSIAN BATTLEMENTS

Long-forgotten war defences

www.jt-line.fi/eng/suomenlinna-vallisaari-lonna/timetable-vallisaari/
Accessible May—September by ferry from Market Square
See website for timetable and Finnish citizens

Tourists visiting King's Gate in Suomenlinna often wonder about the green island across the water. This is Vallisaari, equally rich in military tradition, having served both Russian and Finnish forces. Accessible via ferry from the Market Square between May and September, the 20-minute hop through the scenic archipelago gives a very different experience compared to touristy Suomenlinna. The uninhabited island is not only the natural habitat of rare fauna such as butterflies and bats, but it is also marked with a distinctive human history.

Until relatively recently, the archipelago of Helsinki had a much stronger military presence. The last military-employed inhabitants and their families withdrew from the islands of Suomenlinna (1972), Isosaari (2010s) and Vallisaari (1996) as the locations were deemed unnecessary

for the armed forces. Before that, Vallisaari was a living community, connected by ferry to nearby Santahamina. Vallisaari is still linked by a causeway to neighbouring Kuninkaansaari.

First developed for military purposes with fortification works in 1811, when Russia was at war with Napoleon, the island is full of old military roads, battlements and barracks, most in the decorative Neo-Byzantine style. They are etched with inscriptions by Russian and Finnish soldiers. The most impressive building on the island is the Aleksanterinpatteri (Alexander's Battery), an 1860s red brick coastal artillery battery named after the Tsesarevich (crown prince) of the time. It offers fantastic sea views of Suomenlinna and Helsinki.

There is a ghost story regarding a Russian officer killed in the Sveaborg Rebellion of 1906 (at that time Suomenlinna was known as Sveaborg). The officer's headless spectre is said to haunt the alley of lime trees along the marked trail "Aleksanterin kierros" ("Alexander's Tour") next to the eponymous battery.

Another sinister place is the "Valley of Death" ("Kuolemanlaakso" in Finnish), where a magazine exploded in July 1937, killing 13 employees. The site is along the marked trail. Soviet sabotage was suspected but never proven. There is a memorial plaque displaying the names of the victims.

THE VESIKKO SUBMARINE

Part of a secret German research programme

Susisaari Island
Suomenlinna
May–August 10am–6pm

Vesikko is a restored Finnish submarine on the south-eastern shore of Susisaari Island. It is the only one remaining in Finland. Between May and August you can step inside and experience the cramped living quarters where twenty men once lived and worked below the waves.

Launched in 1933 in Turku, the submarine was originally part of a secret German research programme for re-armament, which was moved to foreign shores in accordance with the terms of the Versailles Peace Treaty signed after World War I. The Treaty's strict military restrictions were designed to bring Germany to heel by incapacitating its army, and submarines were completely banned under its terms.

A prototype for the German Type II submarines, *Vesikko* was later acquired by the Finnish Government and joined the Navy in 1937. It served in the Winter War and World War II, during which she sank the Soviet merchant ship *Vyborg*, her only true naval victory. After the ceasefire in 1944, *Vesikko* was retired. Finland was banned from operating submarines after the war and thus history repeated itself, the move ironically mirroring the boat's origins as part of the banned German submarine development. *Vesikko* was kept in storage until she was turned into a museum in 1973.

Vesikko was one of five submarines to serve in the Finnish Navy. The other four were three larger Vetehinen-class vessels, *Vetehinen*, *Vesihiisi* and *Iku- Turso*, and the smaller *Saukko*.

> The word *vesikko* is the Finnish name for the European mink; *saukko* means otter; and the rest of the names are from Finnish mythology. None of the other submarines has survived — they were sold to Belgium to be scrapped in 1953.

VESTIGE OF JUHANI AATAMINPOIKA'S CELL

Memories of the worst serial killer in Finnish history

Customs Museum
Suomenlinna B 20 D — Susisaari
040 332 2774 or 040 332 6979 — tullimuseo@tulli.fi
May—August, Tuesday—Sundag 12:30pm—17:30pm
Free entry

After visiting the Customs Museum, which showcases the history of smuggling and the Finnish customs service, go to the last room: a white line and a small plaque are reminders of the worst serial killer known in Finnish history; Juhani Aataminpoika was imprisoned here before his demise. Suomenlinna has always been an island of prisoners; they were present from the very beginning in the form of Swedish construction

workers. The Finnish era saw the island used as a prisoner-of-war camp after the Civil War. There is even a prison on the island today.

Juhani Aataminpoika murdered 12 people between October and November 1849. When he was caught, he was put in a cage and displayed as an example. The white line shows the approximate site of his cage.

After leaving his home at the age of 15, Aataminpoika attempted to make a living as a farmhand and began committing petty crimes. In October 1849 he was put on trial for horse theft, but escaped to begin his bloody journey. He first murdered a married couple, then a man called Kustaa Kratula in Lammi. From Lammi he left to meet his family, but he got in a quarrel with his stepfather, Alexander Bohm, and killed him. Aataminpoika then killed his own mother and half-siblings borne by the couple. Aataminpoika continued to Saimaa, murdering more people, but returned in November to Lammi. He went on a crime spree with his friend Antti Suikko, stealing people's money and beating them up; one old woman died of her wounds.

Juhani Aataminpoika was caught on 20 November 1849 and sentenced to spend the rest of his life in a special prison in Viapori. Imprisoned in a small metallic box, only about a square metre in size, he was chained at the hands, feet and neck, whipped regularly and forbidden from scratching his wounds. In September of 1854 a faux execution was held for Aataminpoika, after which he was publicly tortured to death.

NEARBY
Partially destroyed reliefs of the Kronor   ⑲
Suomenlinna fortress

In Suomenlinna fortress, partially hacked away over the doors of the barracks opposite the church, one can see a relief of the Tre Kronor (Three Crowns) of Sweden. The Russians attempted to erase this evidence of the fort's origin but discontinued the work after they realised the outlines would still be recognisable and their work was in vain. Tre Kronor, the national emblem of Sweden, is three yellow coronets (two above and one below) on a blue background.

It first appeared in the 14th century, originally used by King Magnus IV of Sweden. It is most famously displayed on top of the eponymous Tre Kronor castle in Stockholm. The original name of the fortress, "Sveaborg", was corrupted to "Viapori" in the Finnish tongue. After independence it was changed to "Suomenlinna" (Finland's castle), as the old name was deemed too strong a reminder of the past ("Sveaborg" means "Sweden's castle").

SUOMENLINNA TOY MUSEUM

A real treat

Suomenlinna C 66
040 500 6607
posti@lelumuseo.fi — www.lelumuseo.fi
May—September, daily 11am—5pm; October—April, weekends 11am—4pm;
closed November

There are many museums and historical places in Suomenlinna, but if you know where to look, you are in for a treat. Located in a pastel-coloured wooden villa built by the Russian captain Vasiljev in 1911, Suomenlinna Toy Museum has a good collection of old dolls, teddy bears and other Finnish playthings from the early 1800s through to the 1960s.

The entrance to the museum is a little out of the way and can be easily missed. The historical building itself is beautiful, and apart from the charming array of old toys, the museum owns a unique collection of wartime toys and games, including female dolls dressed in Lotta Svärd uniforms.

Lotta Svärd was a voluntary auxiliary paramilitary organisation for women. Originally formed in 1918, it played a significant role in the Second World War when its members were mobilised to replace men conscripted into the army. "Lottas" served in hospitals, at air raid warning positions and performed other auxiliary tasks in cooperation with the army. Due to Soviet demands, the organisation was suppressed by the Finnish government after the war.

> The museum shop sells vintage-style toys and other souvenirs. There is also a pleasant café called Café Samovarbar.

SUOMENLINNA CHURCH'S LIGHT

The only church in the world doubling as a lighthouse

Suomenlinna C 43
09 2340 6126
Daily 12pm—6pm
Ferry from Market Square

On the fortress island, the church of Suomenlinna has a unique feature not easy to spot if you don't know about it already: this is the only church in the world that doubles as a lighthouse. The light acts as a beacon for both sea and air traffic, giving four short bursts — "H" (for Helsinki) in Morse code. The light is the rear light of a range, with the front light being the Harmaja lighthouse 4.8 km to the south.

The original architect of this former Russian Orthodox church from the 1830s (patron saint Alexander Nevsky) was Konstantin A. Thorn, though much of the Gustavian neoclassicism we see today — named after kings Gustav III and Gustav II Adolf — was accomplished by Einar Sjöström in 1929. Most Finns have forgotten the church ever looked any different.

Finns felt that this architectural and religious Russian influence was an embarrassing reminder of the past for the newly independent nation: the enormous onion domes were removed after independence in 1917 when it was converted to the Lutheran denomination. The tall tower that hosts the lighthouse system was built at this time, as it was discovered to be an effective way to hide the central onion dome within it, which can therefore no longer be seen. It was built square and higher than the original dome. The smaller side cupolas had already been removed in 1918.

On the campanile next to the church hangs the biggest and heaviest bell in the whole country, weighing 6,683 kilograms. It was cast in Moscow in 1885. The lions on the entrance were added after independence as a reminder of the newborn nation.

Suomenlinna's church is among the most popular wedding churches in Helsinki, as many couples feel the pretty islands and romantic sea voyage are perfect for the occasion.

A fence built with bronze cannons and a historical chain

The building is surrounded by a very interesting fence, built in the 1870s from massive bronze cannons dating from the previous century. The iron chain between them was originally a defensive one, used to block enemy ships in the straits. This system has most famously been used on the Golden Horn in Constantinople.

ISLAND OF LONNA

The shameful negotiations of Sveaborg's surrender in 1808

The ferry to Lonna leaves from Cholera Pool every hour during summer
You can also get to the ferry from Suomenlinna
Lonna is also accessible with your own boat
www.jt-line.fi/suomenlinna-vallisaari-lonna/aikataulu-lonna

On a ferry trip to Suomenlinna, visitors pass the little island of Lonna – worth a side trip of its own. Lonna has an interesting history that most are unaware of; it acted as the stage for the shameful negotiations of Sveaborg's (Suomenlinna fortress) surrender in 1808 between admiral Carl Olof Cronstedt (see page 162) and the Russians. At the time, the only resident was an old widow living in a small hut, but when the Russians took the island, they began to develop it for military purposes. They called it Dogovornyi (Negotiations island) after the event with Cronstedt.

The Russians built walls, a guardhouse, a mine factory and even a narrow-gauge railway for transporting products from the mines. The railway begins at the ferry pier and leads to the mine factory. There are two small railway cars still present: one on the waterfront and one on the factory courtyard.

Near the ferry pier, visitors can also see some interesting, rusted memorabilia (such as a crane) from the weapon manufacturing time. During the Sveaborg Rebellion there was so much ammunition left that blowing it up would have laid waste to the whole of Sveaborg and Katajanokka. The rebels considered this, but fortunately backed off when they realised the destruction it would cause.

During the War of Continuation, the island hosted a German degaussing device, used to help Finnish warships avoid magnetic mines. The ships circled around the island in the process, which must have looked curious. The degaussing was needed until the 1960s, when the demining in Finnish waters finally ended. The army left the island in 1999 and it opened to public in 2014.

Today, Lonna is a pleasant island with fewer tourists than Suomenlinna. There is a separate ferry running there during the summertime. The island is much smaller but has great views and is a nice, peaceful destination for picnics and sunbathing.

SABOTAGE SCULPTURE

Wear a work of art in a self-proclaimed micronation

Harakka island
A ferry departs from Ullanlinna pier every 30 minutes
In winter, if the ice is thick enough, one can simply walk to Harakka from Kaivopuisto

Close to the centre of Helsinki, in front of Kaivopuisto Park, lies the small island of Harakka (the Finnish word for magpie). Although unremarkable at first glance, the island is home to one of the rare outdoor sculptures of famous Swiss artist H.R. Giger.

Situated on the highest point of the island, *Sabotage* is a pair of metallic boots stylised in the eccentric and wild style for which Giger is known. The boots are more than simply a decoration; any visitor of Harakka is able to wear them. According to Giger, the boots help the visitor to root himself to the island and become one with the ground.

The sculpture was unveiled in 2003 as a part of the Summit of Micronations, when representatives from around the world gathered in Helsinki. The meeting was one of the largest in the history of micronations and had representatives from such popular micronation phenomena as the Principality of Sealand off the UK shore.

At the time of the summit, a group of micronation enthusiasts, artists and activists also declared the island of Harakka as the territory of

the independent State of Sabotage, the so-called "state in time without national borders". Although the Finnish government didn't respond to their proclamation of independence, Harakka still displays a plaque warning people that they are leaving Finland and entering the State of Sabotage. Harakka also boasts an old barracks built by the Russians in 1908, which currently serves as a nature information centre.

Sabotage: a state founded in 2003

The State of Sabotage was founded in 2003 by Austrian artist Robert Jelinek, when it made its first territorial claim in Harakka. The aim of the project was to promote artistic and social freedom, true unity and universal human values that transcend governments. After claiming Harakka, the state made further territorial claims, such as "Baldrockistan" in Australia and "Trojice" in the Czech Republic, thus becoming a unique country of three territories with no borders between them. Sabotage also issues its own passports and identity cards for its citizens.

Though the State of Sabotage was first intended to "die" after ten years of declaring its independence, curiosity surrounding the project has kept it more or less active, even beyond 2013.

What is a micronation?

A micronation is a small self-declared independent state that is not officially recognised by any country or international organisations. They are usually formed as artistic or political statements, or purely for fun. The State of Sabotage is of the former kind. More serious micronation projects include Liberland – a libertarian state project by the Czech politician Vít Jedlička – and the town of Seborga in Italy, which claims over a thousand years of independence.

The number of micronations around the world is difficult to estimate, but there are at least over a hundred that have at some point claimed independence. Most micronations appear and die very quickly, but some have remained quite stable, even gaining slight recognition from authorities. For instance, the neighbourhood of the so-called freetown of Christiania in Copenhagen has been allowed semi-legal autonomy by the Danish government for decades. The most famous micronation of all is the Principality of Sealand, which claims an offshore platform close to the UK as its territory. Sealand was formed by a British radio pirate and major of the British Army, Paddy Roy Bates. After his death, Bates was succeeded by his son Michael as the Regent of Sealand.

Other micronations close to Helsinki are the Swedish Ladonia – a political and artistic statement by the controversial artist Lars Vilks – and the Republic of Jamtland, an "autonomous culture project" in the middle of Scandinavia.

PIHLAJASAARET

A summer paradise island near the city centre

Frequent ferries from Merisatama and Ruoholahti harbours
May—August 9:30am—9pm

In the open sea in front of the city, the Pihlajasaari islands offer a secluded paradise in the summer months. Connected by a bridge, the Eastern and Western Pihlajasaari islands boast great picnic spots, as well as a sandy beach, far from the fumes of the capital.

The picturesque wooden villas in Western Pihlajasaari originate from Terijoki, in the Karelian Isthmus (now Repino, Russia). Eastern Pihlajasaari has something completely different: an old Russian artillery four-cannon battery and bunkers, part of the Krepost Sveaborg, along with plenty of other military artefacts (though the bunkers remain the only visible proof).

The two islands once had an infamous reputation due to a massacre in 1800; a mad soldier from the nearby Sveaborg fortress, Adolph Adler, murdered fisherman Matts Sundberg, along with his wife and their son.

Later, during the Crimean War in 1855, all the forests on the islands were cut so the enemy (the British Navy) would be unable to use them as cover.

During the midsummer, a traditional bonfire is lit on the beach around 9pm. Called "Juhannus" (after Johannes, or St. John's Day), it is an important national holiday, traditionally celebrated in the countryside with a sauna, bonfire and branches of birch (*koivu*) placed beside the front door. The bonfires were originally lit as protection against evil spirits. The Swedish-speaking Finns of the coastal regions often celebrate this day by erecting a maypole (*midsommarstång* or *majstång* in Swedish).

Although pagan in origin, European midsummer celebrations are associated with the nativity of John the Baptist on 24 June.

In folk magic, the midsummer is among the most potent nights, especially for various fertility rituals. Naked maidens would use charms and peek into a well to see their future husband's reflection. In another tradition, an unmarried woman would collect seven different flowers and place them under her pillow to dream of her future husband. The will-o'-the-wisps (*virvatuli*) were believed to appear and mark lost treasures, particularly to those who found the mythical "fern in bloom" or "fern seed" (ferns are cryptograms, therefore reproducing without flowers or seeds).

KUIVASAARI FORTRESS

A military fortress out on the sea

www.ihalines.fi/suomeksi/saannolliset/kuivasaari.html
Open for guided tour only. See website for details

Located some five kilometres out into the Gulf of Finland, due south of Helsinki and west of the military Isosaari island, Kuivasaari is a fortified island still owned by the Finnish Army. For many years it was the outermost inhabited island in the now uninhabited Helsinki archipelago. The isolation has been a blessing to rare flora and fauna, and for some species this is the only place in Helsinki were they can be found. As many as 400 different kinds of butterflies have been discovered on the island.

Kuivasaari is now one of the few outlying islands of Helsinki that can be visited, although visits must be booked in advance. The tour, hosted by an army veteran, is very informative and highly recommended. You are sure to hear many an interesting story from the time when Kuivasaari was a home to soldiers and army personnel. The restaurant is open during tour visits and offers a rare chance to enjoy a cup of coffee and a cinnamon bun in an authentic old military canteen. The island also hosts a grand collection of historic artillery.

Kuivasaari "dry island" gets its name from the fact that there is no fresh water here. Originally used by fishermen, it was converted in 1896 to military purposes by Imperial Russia and fortified in the 1910s as part of

the Krepost Sveaborg, their coastal fortification system. A number of old coastal artillery guns remain installed here, including a rare and exceptionally heavy 12-inch (305 mm) cannon from the Russian steel factory Obuhov. It is the only remaining example of its kind in the world. During the guided tour you will descend inside the cannon, where you can see the long slides that were used for getting the shells in position. This cannon is still used for ceremonial firing on occasions such as Independence Day.

THE WAR MEMORIALS OF ISOSAARI

One of the most interesting and secret places around Helsinki

www.suomensaaristokuljetus.fi/isosaari/
Ferries run on weekends in June and August, and Tuesday–Sunday in July

In 2017 the beautiful island of Isosaari was opened to the public for the first time in over a century. Almost 10 kilometres from the city centre, it is one of the most interesting (and secret) places around Helsinki.

Fortified by the Russians in 1905 after their naval defeat of Tsushima in the Russo-Japanese War, Isosaari has remained in military use until recent times. Many of the paths and roads that criss-cross the island were built by the Czar over a hundred years ago. They've seen little change since those times; the island is a virtual paradise for nature lovers and military history buffs alike.

Isosaari was used as a concentration camp in the Finnish Civil War. Red prisoners and their Russian allies were kept here in terrible conditions. Almost 360 died of execution, hunger or disease. There's a memorial stone indicating their mass grave along the island's central path.

Isosaari is also the site of the final resting place of Englishman George Quinnell. The grave dates from the Crimean War in 1855, when the Royal Navy occupied the island. Quinnell was killed when Russian artillery bombarded Isosaari from nearby Santahamina. This is the only grave of a hostile English soldier anywhere on Finnish soil.

The ambassador of Great Britain has paid several honorary visits to this lonely resting place, maybe remembering the words of World War I poet Rupert Brooke (1887–1915), often associated with British war cemeteries around the world:

*"If I should die, think only this of me;
That there's some corner of a foreign field
That is for ever England."*

ALPHABETICAL INDEX

ALPHABETICAL INDEX

NOTES

NOTES

NOTES

NOTES

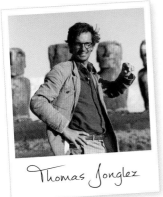

Thomas Jonglez

It was September 1995 and Thomas Jonglez was in Peshawar, the northern Pakistani city 20 kilometres from the tribal zone he was to visit a few days later. It occurred to him that he should record the hidden aspects of his native city, Paris, which he knew so well. During his seven-month trip back home from Beijing, the countries he crossed took in Tibet (entering clandestinely, hidden under blankets in an overnight bus), Iran and Kurdistan. He never took a plane but travelled by boat, train or bus, hitchhiking, cycling, on horseback or on foot, reaching Paris just in time to celebrate Christmas with the family.

On his return, he spent two fantastic years wandering the streets of the capital to gather material for his first "secret guide", written with a friend. For the next seven years he worked in the steel industry until the passion for discovery overtook him. He launched Jonglez Publishing in 2003 and moved to Venice three years later.

In 2013, in search of new adventures, the family left Venice and spent six months travelling to Brazil, via North Korea, Micronesia, the Solomon Islands, Easter Island, Peru and Bolivia. He now lives in Rio de Janeiro with his wife and three children. Jonglez Publishing produces a range of titles in nine languages, released in 30 countries.

ACKNOWLEDGEMENTS

Milla Leskinen

My thanks to all museums, enterprises, associations and archives who have helped me to access sights, information and pictures, especially Helsinki City Museum, Finna.fi, Helsinki Observatory, Jari Markkanen / City of Helsinki Rescue Deparment, Katriina Pyrrö, Teekkarimuseo, Vanha Ylioppilastalo, Suomen Islam-seurakunta, Hotel Klaus K, Juttutupa, Temppeliaukio Church, Reitz Museum, and Signe and Ane Gyllenberg Foundation. I also wish to thank all of my friends who have visited sights with me, gave tips about possible locations and provided aid with the photography, with special thanks to Cem Atel, Arttu Jolma Sidhu, Antti Huttunen, Suvi Karhu, Ira Luostarinen, Sari Toivola and Paula Päivike. Also thanks for my co-author and husband Jiri, in Gandalf's words: "is it secret, is it safe?"

Jiri Keronen

I want to thank all my sages on this mystic path of life, my tribe, my brother and mother; and of course my beloved wife.

PHOTOGRAPHY CREDITS

All photos by **Milla Leskinen**, except these:
Ruttopuisto Park, p. 19: Gunnar Lönnqvist 16.4.1918, Helsinki City Museum; Civil Defence Museum, p. 22–23: Jari Markkanen, The City of Helsinki Rescue Department; Monthly guided tour of the first observatory of Helsinki, p. 30–31: Helsingin observatorio / Helsingin yliopistomuseo; Stepped ravine of Kaivopuisto park, p. 33: Signe Brander 1911, Helsinki City Museum; Carpet washing piers around the centre, p. 35: Bonin von Volker, Helsinki City Museum; The spire of Mikael Agricola Church, p. 37: Viljo Pietinen 1940, Museovirasto / Pietisen kokoelma; Stone in the courtyard of the Burgher's House Museum, p. 41: C.A. Hårdh, circa 1870, Helsinki City Museum; Shrapnel damage in Pitkäsilta bridge, p. 43: Tyyne Böök 12.4.1918, Museovirasto, Historian kuvakokoelma; Ceiling of the National Theatre, p. 46: Kansallisteatteri; *Fossils of Kluuvi Bay* artwork, p. 55: map by N.G Werming, Helsinki City Museum; The coin of Eino Leino's statue, p. 60–61: Cem Atel; *Saga and Truth* statue orientation, p. 62: CreativeCommons, © Jason Jones 2012; Raven statue of Esplanadi, p. 65: Jan Alanco, Helsinki City Museum; Finnish inscription on the Czarina's stone, p. 66: Paula Päivike; Plaque for Eugen Schauman, p. 69: Helsinki City Museum; Medallion of the former Ulrika Eleonora Church, p. 70–71: CreativeCommons, © Heikki Kastemaa; War-damaged artworks in Helsinki University, p. 73: Sotamuseo; Coats-of-arms of the Finnish nobility, p. 84: CreativeCommons, © Matthew Clark; Coats-of-arms of the Finnish nobility, p. 85: K.E. Ståhlberg, SLS; Memorial for mine clearers, p. 89: Suomen merimuseon kuvakokoelma; Stone pillars, p. 93: Signe Brander 1907, Helsinki City Museum; Horse-drawn tram, p. 95: K.E. Ståhlberg 1890's, Helsinki City Museum; Reitz art collection, p. 96–97: Reitz Museum; Bio Rex projection booth stairs, p. 107: Aarne Pietinen 1938, Helsinki City Museum; Yrjönkatu naturist swimming hall, p. 110–111: Helsingin kaupunki; Zeppelin mast of sokos hotel Torni, p. 113: Helsinki City Museum; Lutheran Church, p. 117: Sotamuseo; Private visit to the Helsinki synagogue, p. 121: Eric Sundström, Helsinki City Museum; Villa Gyllenberg, p. 150–151: Matias Uusikylä / Signe and Ane Gyllenberg foundation; Allotment gardens, p. 181: Helsinki City Museum; Site of the first church in Helsinki, p. 173: Jan Alanco 1983, Helsinki City Museum; Kivinokka's garden, p. 195: Wolfgang Heine 1935, Helsinki City Museum; Statue of Kullervo, p. 185: Museovirasto / Pietisen kokoelma; Revolution table, p. 187: Edvin Holmberg 1918, Museovirasto; Yliskylä's pine tree, p. 214: Antti Huttunen; Oil Silo 468, p. 220: Jussi Helsten; Vesikko submarine, p. 231: Sotamuseo 1941; Island of Lonna, p. 239: Simo Rista 1970, Helsinki City Museum

Cartography: Cyrille Suss — **Design:** Emmanuelle Willard Toulemonde — **Editing:** Matt Gay — **Proofreading:** Kimberly Bess and Eleni Salemi — **Publishing:** Clémence Mathé